THE VISION OF
THE BUDDHA

LIVING WISDOM

THE VISION OF THE BUDDHA

TOM LOWENSTEIN

SERIES CONSULTANT: **PIERS VITEBSKY**

DBP

DUNCAN BAIRD PUBLISHERS

LONDON

The Vision of the Buddha

First published in Great Britain in 1996 by Macmillan Reference Books

Conceived, created and designed by Duncan Baird Publishers.
This edition published by
Duncan Baird Publishers
Sixth Floor
Castle House
75–76 Wells Street
London W1P 3RE

A CIP catalogue record (Macmillan Reference Books) for this book is available from the British Library

ISBN 1 900131 20 X

10 9 8 7 6 5 4 3 2

Editors: Roger Hearn, Lucy Rix, Kirsty Seymour-Ure
Designers: Sue Bush, Gabriella Le Grazie
Picture research: Cee Weston-Baker
Cartographic design: Line + Line

Typeset in Times NR MT
Colour reproduction by Colourscan, Singapore
Printed in Singapore by Imago Publishing Limited

Contents

Introduction

The *dharma*, or doctrine, as taught by the Buddha Shakyamuni (Sage of the Shakya people) in the 6th century BC, is one of the world's great religions, with a history of some 2,500 years. Originating in north India, Buddhism spread, in its first thousand years, through Sri Lanka, China, Southeast Asia, Japan and Tibet. The Buddha himself predicted, in harmony with his vision of the impermanence of existence, that his teaching would decline at certain periods before reviving again. In this context, it is striking that whereas the *dharma* has declined in parts of Asia, it has now taken root in Europe and North America.

While Western interest in Buddhism has grown conspicuously since the late 1960s, the *dharma* remains an Eastern religion. What accounts for Buddhism's appeal to the Westerner? Perhaps most importantly, the Buddha – often described as the "great physician" – offers a diagnosis of the suffering experienced by all human beings, and outlines a way of life that leads, through individual effort, to the resolution of that suffering. Secondly, the Buddhist path contains a lofty moral code based on compassion and non-violence, without requiring faith in a deity that, increasingly, Westerners have found hard to imagine. In the practice of meditation, Buddhism offers a simple and accessible, although demanding, means for self-healing, which can lead to tranquillity and to spiritual insight. Finally, Buddhism, in its many forms, is intellectually stimulating, with an immense and varied artistic heritage. That Buddhism has entered Western religious, intellectual and aesthetic life is therefore unsurprising.

But what is Buddhism? Is it the teachings outlined

in the early Pali scriptures (see p.71); the lofty, complex *dharma* of Tibet; or the fiercely demanding vision of Zen? The aim of this book is to offer an account of Indian Buddhist thought and then to trace how this was developed by the Buddha's successors throughout Asia; each chapter covers significant areas of Buddhist practice in the principal regions in which Buddhism evolved.

The final chapter reviews the way in which Buddhism has entered Western society, from its introduction in the 19th century to its contemporary forms in Europe and North America. Most of the classical traditions of Buddhism are represented, and Western practitioners, with the guidance of Oriental masters, have now established monasteries and meditation centres beyond the boundaries of Asia. Inward-looking as Buddhism may at first appear, most Buddhists find that their practice frees them to connect with the world in ways that are lively, confident and direct. As an expression of this, Western Buddhists are increasingly involved in projects serving the homeless, those with AIDS, prison inmates and, not least, the well-being of the environment. Buddhism teaches the connectedness of all beings. It also recognizes their inevitable suffering. But the power of the *dharma* lies in its capacity to alleviate that suffering through the development of wisdom and compassion as taught by the Buddha.

The Svayambhunath stupa *(Buddhist reliquary) in Kathmandu, Nepal.* Stupas *originated in India and recur throughout Buddhist Asia. They are symbols of the Buddha's complete accomplishment. The unique inlaid "all-seeing" eyes of this* stupa *add the notion of the Buddha's wisdom: the vision of reality and compassion achieved in his enlightenment meditation.*

The Early Days of the Buddha

Most religions have stories that describe the origin of the world or the birth and exploits of gods and heroes. And many Asian religions such as Hinduism and Buddhism draw on one anothers' traditions, thus offering the modern mind a sense of the interconnection of ancient ideas. In the way of many major religions, early Buddhist legends owe much to folk traditions. The stories surrounding the Buddha's birth therefore became "Buddhist" perhaps only when they were later appropriated by Buddhists themselves. Much Buddhist doctrine likewise emerges from a shared context. The belief that rebirth was linked to *karma* (past actions) was growing in 6th-century BC India. Also common was the assumption that an escape from rebirth lay in asceticism; that by abandoning conventional society, one could step onto a path leading to salvation. Such ideas arose out of a perception of life's unsatisfactoriness, and the inherent corruption of the mind-body complex. If the body could be restrained and the mind purified, knowledge of ultimate values would be achieved, thus bringing release from the suffering of rebirth. Aspects of these beliefs underpinned the Buddha's thought: but his genius lay in his diagnosis of how, despite the constraints of a gloomy cosmos, an ethical happiness could be realized in this world.

A 14th-century fresco from Wat Phra Tadt Suted temple in Thailand, depicting the Buddha being offered food to sustain him through his long period of meditation.

The Four Sights

The Sanskrit and Pali word *buddha* means "awakened, enlightened". It is, therefore, only after his enlightenment (see pp.24–5) that Siddhartha can be called the Buddha. More frequently he is referred to as the Bodhisattva (an "enlightenment being" destined for *nirvana*). There are few legends of the Bodhisattva's childhood. Most accounts move almost directly from birth to the moment of his decision to leave home to explore the nature of existence.

A 10th-century AD Chinese painting, from Dunhuang, showing Siddhartha and his groom at the start of his great departure from the court.

This "great departure" had been predicted by Suddhodana's *brahmins* (priests). With this in mind, the king – afraid to lose the heir to his kingdom – found Siddhartha a wife, Yasodhara. He also confined the prince to the upper storeys of the palace, where women musicians "delighted him with their soft voices and playful intoxications".

But Siddhartha was restless to see the world. The king allowed his son an excursion into the royal park, but forbade the appearance of afflicted people on the road to the gardens.

The gods (who play a peripheral role in Buddhist legend) seized the opportunity to show Siddhartha a sign. They changed one of their number into a decrepit old man, and showed the old man to the future Buddha. "Friend," the Bodhisattva asked his driver, "who is this man?" At the explanation of old age, he cried, "Shame on birth, since everyone who is born must grow old." And he went home without visiting the park.

A fresco of the Bodhisattva encountering the Four Sights, from Wat Phra Tadt Suted temple, Chiang Mai, Thailand, dating from AD1383.

Similar events took place on further excursions. On

THE GREAT DEPARTURE

Siddhartha saying goodbye to his wife and son before leaving. From a 14th-century AD fresco in Wat Phra Tadt Suted temple, Thailand.

Siddhartha's wife bore him a son, Rahula. But this only strengthened Siddhartha's decision to leave. He heard a woman celebrating the royal happiness in song. "Certainly, happiness is what I am looking for. I must today leave the world in search of happiness."

That evening brought the final sight which would provoke Siddhartha's flight. Dozing among his women musicians, he awoke to find them asleep around him. "Some lay with their bodies wet with phlegm; some ground their teeth, and muttered in their sleep; some lay with their mouths open; others lay with their clothes in disarray to reveal their nakedness. The splendid apartment began to seem like a cemetery filled with dead bodies. 'How oppressive and stifling it all is!' he exclaimed." And summoning his chariot-driver and his horse, he started to leave the palace. But before his departure – "to win for himself the deathless state of *nirvana*" – he visited Yasodhara's apartments. "Within the chamber lay his wife with her hand resting on the boy's head. 'If I were to raise my wife's hand, she would wake and stop me going,' said the prince. 'First I will achieve enlightenment, and then come back and see my son.' "

FIRST EXPERIENCE OF MEDITATION

A famous Sanskrit poem describes the prince as having an experience of quasi-enlightenment before the great departure. On one of his excursions, Siddhartha saw some labourers ploughing and noticed the multitude of tiny creatures which had been killed and injured in the furrows. As the prince observed the exhausted bodies of the ploughmen, he was overcome by compassion. Siddhartha then sat down. His mind became still and he reached the concentration of meditation that comes from insight and yields bliss.

"How dreadful that man should, in his ignorance, not pay attention to his fellow creatures who are helplessly enmeshed in birth, suffering and death!" Thus, says the poet, "he gained insight."

his second and third outings, the gods showed the prince apparitions of a sick man and of a man who had died. His final visit brought the sight of a wandering ascetic, a man of tranquillity.

"Who is this?" the prince asked his attendant. "Sir, this is a man who has retired from the world." The thought of such retirement pleased the prince, and he went on until he came to the park.

Despite his father's attempts to shelter him, Siddhartha thus perceived the realities of human suffering, which would lead him eventually to renounce the life of a householder and seek salvation as a wandering ascetic.

Homeless wandering

An 18th-century Burmese manuscript painting showing (bottom left) the Bodhisattva with his two teachers, and (top left) the exhausted Bodhisattva with the five ascetics.

Two main phases led to the Bodhisattva's enlightenment. Having renounced domestic life and Brahmanical (Hindu) religion, the Bodhisattva – like many fellow seekers – adopted the life of a beggar, "going forth from home" with shaved head, robe and begging bowl.

The first phase in his ascetic career took him successively to two meditation masters. The first, Alara Kalama, specialized in a mental training for the attainment of the "sphere of nothingness". The second, Uddaka Ramaputra, taught a path of meditation leading to a state of "neither knowing nor not-knowing". The Bodhisattva mastered both techniques quickly, but realized that they took him only part of the way towards the truth he was seeking. Rejecting Uddaka's invitation to remain with him as a teacher, he walked away to continue his task alone.

He then entered the second phase: a period of harsh austerities. Because it was believed that the body and its desires were an obstacle to spiritual realization, almost all religious practice in 6th-century BC India involved some self-denial. It was also believed that difficult, fierce and prolonged ascetic practice generated spiritual energy (*tapas*, mystic heat) which would bring a yogi (spiritual adept) supranormal powers, such as clairvoyance, levitation, and the abilities to heal, become invisible, travel through solids and be in two places at once. These are also powers that the shamans of tribal society claim after their ordeals of initiation. For six years the Bodhisattva, in the company of five other mendicants, starved himself in an effort to bring body and mind under complete control.

"I will carry austerities to the uttermost," thought the Bodhisattva, and tried techniques such as living on one sesame seed or one rice grain a day. Sometimes he took no food at all, and rebuffed the gods when they tried to infuse nourishment through his skin. But six years of austerities – during which his body became completely emaciated and black – were "like time spent trying to tie the air into knots". Coming to the decision that "these austerities are not the way to enlightenment", he went begging in villages and towns for ordinary food and lived upon it. The thirty-two characteristics of a great being again appeared, and "the colour of his body became like gold".

This concluded the second phase of the Bodhisattva's wandering.

A figure of the fasting, emaciated Bodhisattva in a temple near Phnom Penh, Cambodia.

This gilt-bronze statuette in the Pala style shows the Bodhisattva in meditation on a lotus flower.

ASCETISM

In ancient Indian society, ascetic discipline was linked to the development of magical powers. Whereas life within conventional society led to a familiar and ordinary existence, austerities could lead to the development of supranormal powers (*siddhis*). The Buddha contributed moral and perceptual elements to this notion. Firstly, personal restraint is an expression of both awareness and compassion. Secondly, a mind that is preoccupied with pleasure would lack the depth, subtlety and freedom to apprehend reality. But the Buddha also warned against extreme asceticism (see pp.26, 35).

Perceived from outside, Buddhist monastic life still appears ascetic. But monastic discipline for most Buddhist monks is a rich source of happiness, not deprivation.

Karma and *samsara*

Underpinning the Bodhisattva's quest for "the deathless state of *nirvana*" was the theory that people and all other sentient beings were trapped in a repeated series of unsatisfactory births. A common belief among many ancient tribal peoples was that souls transmigrated from one life to another. This meant that after death, human and animal souls might continue to live in the air or water, or go to a communal home of souls awaiting rebirth in either human or animal form. In the 2nd millennium BC, Aryan peoples from the north settled in northwest India and developed the Brahmanical religion from which Hinduism evolved. These people believed in a permanent, deathless afterlife in the "world of the fathers". But by the 7th century BC the doctrine of transmigration, modified by Indian ideas, had returned and was widespread.

The Indian understanding of transmigration in the Buddha's lifetime (*c.* 566–483BC) was known as *samsara*. The Sanskrit word *samsara* literally means "perpetual wandering", and refers to the journey of souls through an infinite and unwelcome number of lives. Even the gods were believed by Buddhists to die, to be replaced by other gods in temporary heavens. This mechanical cycle of death and rebirth was administered in a universe which itself was subject to destruction and re-creation.

Humans and other beings were also governed by a second law which determined their place in these cosmic changes. This was the law of *karma* (literally "work, deed, action"). The doctrine of *karma* taught that all action involved a build-up, in the soul or personality construct, of spiritual merit or de-merit. Good action was followed by merit, and this resulted in favourable rebirth. Bad action, whether or not intentional, led to unfavourable births. But perfect behaviour as a social being – in domestic life, government, trade or even the priesthood – was no guarantee against rebirth. The only path to release from *samsara* was through asceticism. Only the ascetic, living completely detached from social ties and indifferent to the body, could achieve a personal knowledge of life and the spirit that would lead to *nirvana*.

The laws of *karma* and *samsara* can continue today to have psychological potency – for Buddhist and non-Buddhist, and irrespective of rebirth doctrine.

This 10th-century bronze statue from south India depicts the Hindu god Shiva as "King of Dance", with drum and fire in his hands and one foot trampling the dwarf of ignorance. The encircling fire suggests the play of nature which Shiva's dance maintains. But Shiva also destroys, both illusion and the cosmic cycle which is a universalization of the soul's personal experience of samsara. *Hindus and Buddhists thus seek one aim in common: an end to ignorance and rebirth.*

An 18th-century Japanese painting of the Kose school showing the entry of the Buddha into nirvana *with all creation in mourning.* Nirvana *is represented, after the fashion of Pure Land Buddhism, as a kind of heaven.*

NIRVANA

Nirvana was seen by early Buddhists as the only genuine escape from *samsara*. The Sanskrit word *nirvana* means "a blowing out, to become extinguished", like a flame. Although it comes into Hindu scriptures, *nirvana* is primarily a Buddhist term. The purpose of the Hindu or Brahmanical saint was to purify the soul of its *karma* until the soul or self (*atman*) could be experienced as identical with the universal spirit (*brahman*) and the two could be united. The Buddha taught a different doctrine, that of "not-soul" or "not-self" (*anatta*; see pp.28–9). In keeping with this, *nirvana* was a condition only to be experienced by someone who had eliminated the self and any notion of the self. While *samsara* is experienced by everybody all their lives, *nirvana* is beyond ordinary words or concepts; in the Buddha's words, it is: "Peace. The absolute. The end of the construct of the human personality. The end of every trace that could be reborn. The death of craving. Detachment. Extinction." And just as *samsara* concerns continual rebirth, *nirvana* is "unborn, unoriginated, uncreated, unformed. If the unborn, uncreated, unformed did not exist, escape from the world of the born, created and formed would not be possible."

The Enlightenment

Narratives of the Buddha's enlightenment fall into two main parts. The first is filled with inner struggle as the future Buddha mortifies his body and is then assaulted in the initial stages of his enlightenment meditation by the "evil one". Though this phase is expressed in folkloric form, it is an intensely human story. The Buddha is not represented as superhuman; no revelatory light is suddenly switched on for him. Enlightenment occurs only when he has witnessed and transcended the darkness of universal negativity. The second phase takes place in a serenity which is therefore achieved rather than given.

The Buddha's freedom from self and knowledge of truth – a condition described as *nirvana* – arises from within his hard-won equanimity. It is at this moment that the Bodhisattva (future Buddha) becomes Buddha (one who has woken). The knowledge revealed in his meditation becomes the heart of his doctrine: the Middle Way. This way is a path of no extreme; it demands recognition of "things as they are". It enshrines the four truths about human suffering that underlie all Buddhist teaching. These early Buddhist formulations are easy enough to comprehend intellectually. But subjective understanding of the Buddhist revelation requires investigation, study and meditation.

Devotees have laid marigolds in the footprints of the Buddha at Bodh Gaya, site of the Buddha's enlightenment experience; the Buddha was never depicted as a man in early Indian representation. Here, the two feet are enclosed by stylized lotus petals, suggesting they rise from the lotus of wisdom and purity.

The struggle for enlightenment

The Bodhisattva had arrived at the Nairanjana River, a tributary of the Ganges. He knew the time had come for the final stage in his quest for enlightenment. In 531BC, he was thirty-four years old, and had absorbed three major spheres of experience: the exaggerated luxury of palace life, the teaching of two great yogis and, lastly, extreme asceticism. He had renounced them all. But a reflection of each was built into the knowledge from which his enlightenment would spring.

Near a place called Uruvela, the Bodhisattva stopped to seek a suitable place for meditation. It was the day of full moon, and a young woman called Nandabala wished to make an offering to the sacred pipal tree which, unknown to her, the Bodhisattva had chosen as the site of his meditation. Carrying a dish of milk-rice, the young woman walked to the river bank, where, at the foot of the tree, she found the future Buddha. Perceiving that he was a holy man, she made her offering directly to him. "May your wishes prosper like my own," she said, and departed. The future Buddha rose, walked around the tree in a sunwise (clockwise) direction, bathed in the river, returned to his seat at the eastern side of the tree and ate the rice. Vowing to remain there until he had attained enlightenment, he sat cross-legged on his "throne of wisdom" and for the next forty-nine days neither moved nor took food.

An empty seat below the bodhi *(enlightenment) tree symbolizes the Buddha. He is protected by the serpent deity Muchalinda.*

The enlightenment was preceded by a vision of demonic intensity in the shape of an assault by Mara, the "evil one", "enemy of *dharma*". The figure of Mara was identified by early Buddhists with Kama, the Hindu god of sensuality. It was in this guise that Mara, with flower-tipped arrows that excite desire and accompanied by his three sensual daughters, attempted to seduce the Bodhisattva from his concentration. This proving futile, Mara appealed to the prince's sense of duty: "Rise, O warrior! Follow the *dharma* [path] of your caste. Renounce the *dharma* of liberation! It is unworthy for a prince to live as a beggar."

Infuriated by the failure of more or less subtle temptations, Mara then unleashed his army to undermine the Bodhisattva's tranquillity. Grotesque demons – some speckled, deformed and with pendulous bellies, some with twisted, half-

A detail from a 19th-century cloth wall banner from Thailand, depicting the Buddha's victory over Mara, the "evil one".

gnawed faces, some garmented in snakes, bristling, leaping, speeding through the tree-tops, with their hairs spouting fire – crowded the root of the pipal tree. Then night came down. There were violent winds and the earth was convulsed. But the Bodhisattva was no more alarmed by Mara's demons than he would have been by over-excited infants playing. The demons were enraged. They hurled rocks, trees, axes and blazing logs the size of mountains. Winds reduced towns and villages to powder. There were showers of hot coals, of flaming mountain-tops, double-edged weapons, sand, mud, and then further darkness. But the Bodhisattva's self-possession and compassion checked Mara's weapons in mid-flight or transformed them into showers of lotus petals.

"Siddhartha!" cried Mara "Arise from that seat! It belongs to me."

"Mara," replied the Bodhisattva, "you have not laboured for knowledge, nor the world's welfare, nor for enlightenment. This seat does not belong to you, but to me." This seat of wisdom was that on which all past Buddhas-to-be had won enlightenment (see pp.22–3).

"But who," asked Mara, "will bear witness to the dedication of your past lives and their generosity?"

Having no other witness than the place where he sat, the Bodhisattva extended his hand and touched the earth. At this the earth thundered, "I bear witness!" Mara was defeated.

Recollection of past lives

After the storm of "Mara's war" (see pp.20–21), the Bodhisattva entered the deep, untroubled meditation that he had spontaneously experienced when he had seen the ploughmen (see p.13). In the clarity of this new sphere he perceived his own place in the history of all *bodhisattvas* and Buddhas, and recollected his own past lives.

The theory of rebirth was almost universal in ancient India and it underlies much Buddhist legend. In harmony with the theory was the Indian belief that the cosmos goes through innumerable cycles of destruction and re-creation. Everything that dies in universal conflagration is reborn in a new era to repeat its previous existence. Every human action likewise repeats a previous action. This is the notion behind the Bodhisattva's statement that his "seat of wisdom" had been the seat of previous *bodhisattvas*. The Buddha of history – who was born into the same cosmic era as we inhabit today – was thus only the latest in a series of past and future Buddhas. One Buddha of remote legendary time was Dipankara. The last Buddha before Siddhartha was Kashyapa. The Buddha of the future will be Maitreya who is believed to exist already as a compassionate *bodhisattva*.

Just as there is a series of Buddhas who are identical in all but their personal names, so each Buddha must go through many births as a Buddha-to-be

THE *JATAKA* "BIRTH STORIES"

Most *Jataka* tales are based on pre-Buddhist folk stories with refreshingly worldly "morals". In one, the Bodhisattva is born as a monkey who one day meets a crocodile "with a longing to eat his heart". Using his wits to escape the predator, by persuading him that he keeps his heart hanging on a nearby fig tree, the monkey exclaims: "You foolish crocodile. Your body is great, but you have no sense. Go your ways: for I've had the best of it!"

"I was that monkey," says the Buddha who ostensibly tells this lively trickster story.

Other *Jataka* tales illustrate more recognizable Buddhist virtues. There is the story of the monkey (another *bodhisattva*) who laid his body across the Ganges, exposing himself to death so that his companions could escape a party of hunters. Other examples of self-sacrifice are provided by creatures as diverse as tigers, goats and rabbits who are future Buddhas. Many such *Jataka* stories are versions of animal fables found in cultures as diverse as Greek, Native North American and Inuit (Eskimo).

Scenes from the Buddha's life, as described in Jataka *stories, are shown in this carved limestone relief, from the 1st-century* AD *Amaravati* stupa, *Andhra Pradesh.*

This page from a mid-19th-century illustrated book of the Jatakas *in Burmese depicts a scene from the Buddha's previous birth as a tree spirit.*

(*bodhisattva*) before he reaches his last and most exalted incarnation. Approximately 550 "birth stories" (*Jatakas*) in the Pali Buddhist canon (see p.71) describe the lives of the *bodhisattva* who became Siddhartha Gautama. Perhaps the most famous is the *brahmin* Sumedho, a follower of the Buddha Dipankara, who humbly spread his hair before Dipankara so his feet would not be soiled as he walked. The story records how Dipankara foresaw that Sumedho would ultimately be reborn as Siddhartha.

Many *Jataka* stories focus on a particular act of overwhelming altruism to illustrate the Buddha's "perfection of generosity". The best known of these is the tale of Prince Vessantara, the Bodhisattva's last incarnation before he became Siddhartha. In a gesture of supreme selflessness, Vessantara gave away his children, then his wife, to wandering *brahmins*. The ethical ambiguity of these gifts is to some extent resolved when we learn that the second *brahmin* was the god Sakka (Indra), come to test Vessantara's generosity.

The Buddha's enlightenment

After the metaphysical drama of the Mara episode and the mystery of the Bodhisattva's recollection of his previous lives, descriptions of the Buddha's enlightenment are quiet, humanistic and relatively straightforward. Philosophy and a psychological ethic replace myth and legend. The image of the supernatural hero at a climax of universal time gives way to that of a man in the forest, deep in thought and meditation on the nature of human experience.

There are, in the Pali texts (see p.71), several accounts of the Bodhisattva's meditation, and most of them divide the night of his enlightenment into three periods or "watches". In the first watch the Bodhisattva recalls his past lives. In the second watch he analyses the law of *karma*: "With mind composed, I directed my mind to the knowledge of the death and rebirth of beings. I comprehended that beings are lowly, excellent, well-destined or ill-fated according to the consequence of their actions." In the third watch the Bodhisattva arrives at the three basic components of the Buddhist *dharma* (doctrine): the Four Noble Truths, the Three Characteristics of Existence (see pp. 28–9) and the Law of Causality (see pp.30–31). With these revelations, Siddhartha is freed from rebirth and *samsara*. He enters a living *nirvana* and becomes a Buddha.

The Four Truths are described as "noble [*aryan*] truths" because they are exalted. However simple they may at first appear, they may be comprehended fully only by those who have embarked on the "serious" or "noble" quest. The truths, as recorded in the Pali texts, are set out by the Buddha in the following passage:

A 17th–18th-century representation of the bodhi *tree under which the Buddha gained enlightenment, from Ayutthaya, Burma. The beautiful heart-shaped leaves are naturalistically depicted.*

"What, monks, is the truth of suffering [*dukkha*; see p.28]? Birth is suffering, decay, sickness and death are suffering. To be separated from what you like is suffering. To want something and not get it is suffering. In short the human personality, liable as it is to clinging and attachment, brings suffering.

The seated Buddha with his hands in the teaching posture: a sublime work of 5th-century AD Gupta carving. The Buddha as the exemplar of human perfection is depicted by stone-carvers from perhaps the greatest period of north Indian carving.

"And what is the truth of the origin of suffering? It is craving. Craving leads to rebirth, bound up as this is with the search for pleasure and restless greed. It is in craving for sensuality, craving for new life, craving for non-existence and annihilation.

"And what is the truth of the extinction of suffering? It is the indifference to and elimination of craving: freedom and detachment from it.

"And what is the truth about the Way [or the Path] leading to the extinction of suffering? Just this excellent Eightfold Path that leads to the extinction of suffering:

"Right view. Right thought [or purpose].

"Right speech. Right action. Right livelihood.

"Right effort. Right awareness [or mindfulness]. Right meditative concentration."

THE BODH GAYA SHRINE

For more than 2,000 years Uruvela (now Bodh Gaya, "where wisdom was acquired") has been a great Buddhist site. Soon after the Buddha's death, Bodh Gaya became a centre of pilgrimage with monasteries, shrines and *stupas* (reliquaries). Today, with its *bodhi* tree said to be a descendant of the original tree, Bodh Gaya is again a thriving Buddhist centre.

Other shrines sprang up in the early Buddhist period. One tradition suggests that the Buddha meditated under at least three trees, for a week each. Under the first he meditated on the the Law of Causality; under the second he conversed with a *brahmin*. During the third week, in a violent storm, the Buddha sat under the "Muchalinda tree" and the serpent king Muchalinda protectively enfolded his body.

The greatly restored Mahabodhi temple at Bodh Gaya dates from the 7th century.

The Middle Way

The apotheosis of sexual love, shown in a 10th–11th-century Hindu temple carving from Khajuraho, Madhya Pradesh. The Buddhist Tantra later appropriated such iconography.

The Buddha's enlightenment took place on the middle ground between the two major areas of his previous experience: the extreme sensuality that was forced on him by court life, and the equally extreme asceticism of his six years with the five mendicants. While the tale of Nandabala's offering of milk-rice (see pp. 20–21) may be legendary, the point of the story is crucial. The Buddha had already chosen his place of meditation because it was peaceful and pleasant. Well-nourished, having taken the rice, he could then sit in a happy posture with the right energy for thought and meditation.

The Eightfold Path is itself at the heart of the Middle Way. Concluding the Four Truths, the Eightfold Path is divided into three parts. Right view and right thought lead to wisdom. Right speech, right action and right livelihood lie in the sphere of ethics. Right effort, right awareness and right concentration belong to the practice of meditation.

The word "right" can be interpreted in three main ways. First is doctrinal correctness: a "right view or understanding" of the Four Great Truths. Secondly, in the ethical sense the word "right" dictates non-violence and honesty in speech, thought and action. In a third respect, "right" suggests balance: a skilfully manoeuvred middle way. "Right effort" in following the path may thus refer to strenuous effort balanced with the insight which avoids fanaticism, bigotry and self-punishment. Right awareness and concentration are in balance with each other. Right awareness (*sati*) is a heightened, non-judgmental, non-self-centred, moment-to-moment attention to the Buddhist path, to everyday action and to others. Continuous mindfulness is open, flexible, mobile: it accompanies each moment of life, whether painful,

A roundel from Amaravati (Madhya Pradesh, 2nd century AD) showing King Suddhodana visiting Mahamaya at the time of the Bodhisattva's birth. In contrast to the erotic tension of the couple opposite, these figures impart

a calm self-possession. From the matrix of this harmonious collective dharma *– relaxed, naively charming, devoid of visible religiosity – the adult Buddha would emerge with the* dharma *of insight and compassion.*

neutral or full of delight. "Concentration" (*samadhi*), by contrast, is "one-pointed". It is consciousness narrowed to a chosen focus: an elimination of distraction, a coming together of otherwise scattered mental activity. Outgoing awareness thus balances the inner stillness of *samadhi* which is necessary for the development of wisdom. Without the tranquillity of *samadhi*, the deeper truth will be obscured by mental chatter, anxiety and shallow psychological concerns.

The Buddha's remedy for eliminating the craving that underlies suffering is the Eightfold Path. "Rightly" followed, the path provides an exit from the treadmill of *samsara* (the cycle of rebirth). The Buddha is himself the exemplar of this process. On his enlightenment, he became free of craving, *dukkha* (suffering) and ego. Birth had been transcended. This is the "unborn", absolute sphere of *nirvana*: the fruit of observing the Eightfold Path which is at the heart of the Middle Way. It is a path still taken today by countless Buddhists in Asia and the West.

THE SEVEN FACTORS OF ENLIGHTENMENT

At the hour of his death, the Buddha summarized the whole of his teaching in thirty-seven essential aspects. The major groups in the summary were the Eightfold Path, the Four Foundations of Awareness and the Seven Factors of Enlightenment. Some of these seven correspond to the Eightfold Path. They are as follows: awareness, investigation of the *dharma*, energy, joy, tranquillity, concentration and equanimity. Developing and perfecting these, the practitioner can achieve the status of *arhat* (enlightened person) and so arrive at *nirvana*.

Noble, elegant, relaxed and secure: this rock-cut meditating Buddha from Polonnaruwa (Sri Lanka, 12th century) epitomizes the unshakeable happiness of the Buddhist path.

The Three Characteristics of Existence

A 9th-century relief from Borobudur (Java) showing a merchant's encounter with nymphs. Legend is given naturalistic treatment. Myth and nature, the timeless and the temporal, converge in a vision of transience and ambiguity in a complex, quintessentially Buddhist image of existence.

Dukkha (see p.25) is a difficult term to translate, and most Western writers use a word like "suffering" as a convenient shorthand. But to bring out its flavour fully, the word *dukkha* must be contemplated as a personal reality until fresh words and non-verbal perceptions come to help fill out its wider meaning. This is not to suggest that the notion of "suffering" as we ordinarily understand it is unimportant. The world is full of terrible and obvious affliction, and the Buddhist path demands the development of compassion – fellow feeling – for all beings. *Dukkha* does connote physical suffering, and the feelings of grief, depression and despair that were identified by the Buddha. But *dukkha* also suggests the unsatisfactoriness, inconclusiveness and incoherence of most human experience. Even when one is not particularly unhappy, life is a series of incomplete thoughts, relationships and actions. Our lives are short, our experiences transient and fragmentary.

A major part of *dukkha* lies in this factor of impermanence. And impermanence (*anicca*) as an adjunct to *dukkha* is the second of life's three characteristics.

The third defining mark of existence is that all phenomena are without self or a soul (*anatta*). The Buddhist *anatta*

doctrine represents a clear break from the Brahmanical (Hindu) belief that the individual soul or self might eventually be united with the world soul. In contrast to this, the Buddha proclaimed that "all things are not-self" (*sabbe dhamma anatta*). There is no abiding soul, self or ego at the centre of the human personality. Human beings are a bundle of five impermanent "heaps" (*skandha*). These are: bodily form, feeling, perception, inherited karmic formations and consciousness. The five *skandhas* cling to the notion of an ego that unites them, but in reality there is nothing there but a series of processes.

NOT-SELF DOCTRINE

Two famous Pali verses (see p.71) sum up the Buddhist theories of personality and not-self:

> When all its constituent parts are there,
> We use the word "cart".
> Likewise, where the "five heaps" exist
> We talk in terms of a "living being".
> (*Samyutta Nikaya*)

> Suffering exists. But not the sufferer.
> The act is done. But there is no doer.
> Peace exists. But not the one who is at peace.
> There is a path. But no one walks it.
> (Buddhaghosa, *Visuddhimagga*)

Combining these two points of view is the tale of the nun Vajira who was tormented with doubts by the evil Mara: "What is a 'person'? How does he arise? Who creates him?"

Vajira answered: "Mara, why do you insist on the word 'person'? There is nothing here but a group of processes. Just as the word 'cart' is used when the parts are combined, so the word 'person' is commonly used when the five *skandhas* are present."

The plantain tree with its pithless stem is a Buddhist symbol of impermanence.

The Law of Causality

The Tibetan Wheel of Becoming represents the Buddhist universe and the doctrine of causality. Six rebirth destinies – in hell, as animals, ghosts, gods, titans and humans – are shown within the spokes. Lust, hatred and stupidity (a mutually attached dove, snake and pig) are shown in the middle. Clutching the Wheel as though to swallow it, is a monster representing impermanence. Beyond samsara, *at the top, the Buddha points to* nirvana. *The Wheel of Becoming derived from a vision of the Buddha's disciple Maudgalyayana. The design probably travelled to Tibet in the 8th century* AD.

The Buddha's other central revelation under the *bodhi* tree (see pp. 24–5) was his theory of causality or "dependent origination". In this, he showed that every aspect of human life is conditioned by a prior influence or state of being. Nothing exists in its own right: it comes into being on account of something else and then passes. The assumption from which this doctrine begins is that there is suffering, disease, old age and death. But how do these conditions arise? And how can they be eliminated? The Buddha concludes that suffering arises as a result of personal *karma* (past action). But *karma* accumulates only on account of ignorance.

The chain of causality is as follows:

Because of ignorance, rebirth-producing-*karma*-formations arise; because of rebirth-producing-*karma*-formations, consciousness arises; because of consciousness, name-and-form (mental and physical phenomena) arise; because of name-and-form, the sense spheres arise; because of the sense spheres, contact arises; because of contact, feeling arises; because of feeling, craving arises; because of craving, clinging arises; because of clinging, the process of becoming arises; because of becoming, rebirth arises; because of rebirth, old age, death, pain, grief and despair arise.

But the process can be reversed. When the knowledge of enlightenment is achieved, *karma* and suffering are eliminated; and the fear of death is replaced with the possibility of *nirvana*.

The Wheel of Becoming traditionally depicts the stages of causation in the outer rim: ignorance (a blind man); karma *formation (a potter); consciousness (a monkey); name and form (a ship with passengers); the senses (an empty house); contact (a man and woman embracing); feeling (a man gathering fruit); becoming (a woman and child); birth (a woman in childbirth); old age and death (a man with a corpse).*

THE BUDDHA'S COMPASSION

The Sanskrit poem *The Acts of the Buddha* emphasizes compassion as an element of the enlightenment: "After recalling his past births and deaths, the Buddha was filled with compassion for all beings. 'Truly there is no hope for the world; it just spins like a wheel.' As he considered the past, his conviction grew that the cycle of existence, like the pithless stem of a plantain tree, lacked any substance. Then with purified vision, he beheld the world, as if in a mirror. His compassion grew as he saw the death and rebirth of all beings according to their *karma*." The poet here uses two common Buddhist images. The wheel, otherwise symbolizing the orderly *dharma*, is pictured spinning on an overturned cart. The banana tree trunk, lacking heartwood, is a symbol of impermanence and not-self (see pp.28–9).

From Enlightenment to Death

The biography of the Buddha after his enlightenment describes new areas of experience. Earlier accounts abounded in supranormal elements; these now dwindle, and much of the rest of the Buddha's lifetime is recounted naturalistically. In the dusty towns and cooling orchards of the Ganges basin, the Buddha and the princes, *brahmins* and artisans with whom he consorted become palpably real historical characters. We hear the Buddha's voice: persistent in his teaching and sometimes sharp-tongued with opposition. For a teacher who proclaimed the non-existence of the ego, the Buddha was a powerful personality, and it is interesting to observe how his universal vision is proclaimed through the towns and villages of small northeastern Indian kingdoms. This period sees the emergence of major followers. But the Buddha's was not the only new voice in the meeting places of 6th-century BC India. Other religious thinkers – *brahmins*, Jains, yogis, nihilists – offered alternative ideas.

Finally, with absolute tranquillity, the Buddha nears the *parinirvana* (completed *nirvana*). The Master's approach to death is a major aspect of his doctrine. While the dying teacher enjoins equanimity, the story itself is deeply moving.

The Buddha in parinirvana *with his attendant Ananda, from the 12th-century group of statues at Polonnaruwa, Sri Lanka. The serene and yet vividly alive quality of the carving is enhanced by the rock-grain which flows horizontally across the vertical Ananda and suffuses the rhythm of the draperies of both figures.*

After the enlightenment

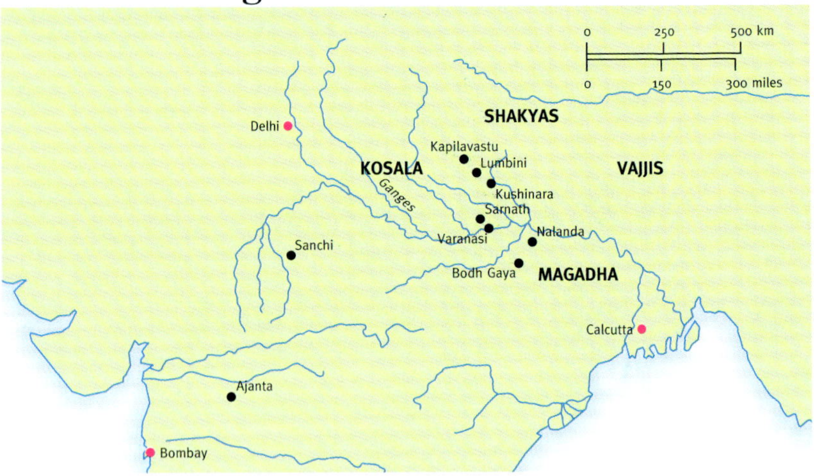

A map of northern India at the time of the Buddha, showing important Buddhist sites, with three modern cities indicated in pink.

The essence of the Buddha's teaching (*dharma*) is contained in his enlightenment. "Having understood *dukkha*," says one text, "the Master delivered this utterance: 'When the real nature of things becomes clear in meditation, the *brahmin* [wise man] knows things and their causes.'" In Buddhism, the phrase "the real nature of things" is vital. Humanity had laboured under illusions about the nature of self and the means of escaping *samsara*. Re-entering the world after his enlightenment meditation, the Buddha was sure that his vision of suffering and impermanence was the true reality.

This 12th-century Burmese figure shows the god Brahma, the creator, who encouraged the Buddha to teach.

But there were, after the enlightenment, certain difficulties to be overcome. The Buddha had wandered into the kingdom of Magadha about 200 miles (320km) southeast of his homeland. He belonged neither to the religious orthodoxy nor to any established group of yogis such as surrounded his first two teachers. His new version of reality set him still further apart. Pali texts (see p.71) portray him as being conscious of his apartness:

"I had discovered this subtle and profound truth, difficult to perceive, inaccessible to rational thought." Perhaps it would be futile trying to convey his vision to a world where most lived in delusion.

Another text describes his dilemma thus: "When he saw on the one side the world lost in low views and confused efforts ... and saw on the other the exceeding subtlety of the *dharma* that leads to freedom, he felt inclined to take no action. But when he considered the pledge that he had taken in past lives to enlighten all beings, he grew more favourable to the idea of proclaiming the path that leads to peace."

According to legend, the Buddha's resolution was strengthened by the god Brahma, who urged him: "Now that you, O sage, have yourself crossed the ocean of the world of becoming, please rescue the other living beings who have sunk so low in suffering."

Thus the Buddha set out to teach.

THE BUDDHA REDEFINES THE WORD *BRAHMIN*

One text reports that while the Buddha was meditating "in the happiness of emancipation", he was visited by a *brahmin* (person of the priestly high caste) who asked, "What constitutes a *brahmin*?"

"A true *brahmin*," replied the Buddha, "is one who has conquered evil in himself: one who is free from pride, restrained and virtuous. He alone may call himself a *brahmin*."

To deny the validity of inherited caste status was a revolutionary concept in ancient India. In the text quoted opposite, the Buddha talked of the "meditating *brahmin*". Here also we find the Master using *brahmin* in a new way. In the Buddha's view, it was personal *karma* and right effort, not caste or class, that distinguished people. The Buddha consorted with people from every sphere of north Indian society. Two prominent individuals to offer him the daily meal were a courtesan and a blacksmith.

THE BUDDHA ENCOUNTERS THE FIVE ASCETICS

The Buddha's first encounter after his enlightenment was at Sarnath, near Varanasi, with the five men who had been his companions of earlier austerities. On meeting the enlightened Buddha, all they saw was an ordinary man: they mocked his well-nourished appearance. "Here comes the mendicant Gautama," they said, "who has turned away from asceticism. He is certainly not worth our respect." When they reminded him of his former vows, the Buddha replied, "Austerities only confuse the mind. In the exhaustion and mental stupor to which they lead, one can no longer understand the ordinary things of life, still less the truth that lies beyond the senses. I have given up extremes of either luxury or asceticism. I have discovered the Middle Way."

A painting by a modern Burmese artist depicting the Buddha's First Sermon ("the First Turning of the Wheel of Law") to the five ascetics in the deer park at Sarnath. This was the discourse on the Four Noble Truths and the Middle Way, which converted the five mendicants from their extreme asceticism to become the first members of the Buddha's community.

The social and religious context

Sixth-century BC India, like Greek society of the same period, was in a state of profound social change and philosophical revolution. In the lands watered by the Ganges, new monarchal states, such as Kosala and Magadha, were expanding. The Pali scriptures, the main source of our knowledge of the Buddha's milieu (see p.71), abound with kings, noblemen, priests, merchants and philosophers, conveying a sense of bustle, money, patronage and creativity. Above all, there was a ferment of intellectual inquiry and restless philosophical debate.

A 5th-century AD mural from Ajanta, Maharashtra, depicting the bodhisattva *prince Mahajanaka. Some of the Buddha's earlier incarnations as a prince foreshadow his final birth as a* kshatriya, *not a* brahmin.

For the traditional, a bed-rock of religious certainty remained, in Hindu deism or the religious speculations of the *Upanishads*. The latter were the forest teachings of holy men who sought salvation through the unification of the soul (*atman*) with the ultimate reality of the world spirit (*brahman*).

The ritual-based religion of the *brahmins* existed in the regions where the Buddha taught, but its stronghold was in western India. The Brahmanical system emphasized fire sacrifice and social and religious hierarchies based on the Vedic (Hindu) texts. A number of Pali texts show the Buddha in conversation with *brahmins*. In one, a priest outlines the five qualifications for a *brahmin*, who must be: well-born on both sides; able to recite three *Vedas* (holy books); handsome and light-coloured; virtuous; and learned and wise. The Buddha reduces the qualifications for "spiritual aristocracy" to wisdom and virtue (see p.35). Nevertheless, although the Buddha seems to have disregarded caste distinctions, there is no evidence that he actively attempted to break down caste barriers. Many of his followers were from the *kshatriya* (warrior) caste; and it was not until the development of Mahayana in the 1st century AD (see pp.60–61) that Buddhism truly became a popular religion.

While the cities of the 6th century BC swarmed with shifting new populations, the roads were busy with the movement of religious wanderers and teachers with their followers. These were the thinkers who, like the Sophists of 6th-century Greece, renounced the partly myth-based metaphysics of orthodox religion. Many scholars have linked the upsurge in philosophical speculation with the growth of north Indian cities during this period.

THE BUDDHA'S VIEW OF THE HINDU GODS

Early Buddhism is non-theistic. The Buddha himself was a man, and he achieved liberation through his own effort. He worshipped no God or gods; nor was he deified after his death. But the Buddha never denied the existence of gods. Brahma was said to have spoken to him after the enlightenment; and the Buddha referred to deities such as Indra and Mara as a matter of course.

Everyone in 6th-century BC India would have believed in supernatural presences of some kind; yet this was not necessarily to credit them with power, still less with omnipotence. In Buddhist belief, the gods were insignificant presences.

The four-faced Brahma and blue-skinned Vishnu with Shiva and Parvati, from a Shiva temple, Kalahasti, 7th century AD. The Buddha recognized, but took little account of, the ancient deities.

Subject to suffering and rebirth, they lived in heavens that may have been superior to earth. But, partly due to their attachment to sensuality and their blindness to the Four Truths (see p.24–5), they had not entered *nirvana*.

A 1st-century AD carving from Sanchi showing King Bimbisara of Magadha visiting the Buddha. The Buddha was as likely to consort with the poor as with the nobility.

CONTEMPORARY PHILOSOPHERS

In Pali texts we learn of several new philosophers who were contemporaries of the Buddha. Some of these thinkers, like "Ajit of the Hairy Blanket", were materialists. Ajit proclaimed: "Man is formed of the four elements. When he dies earth returns to earth, water to water, and air to air, and his senses vanish in space. Only fools preach almsgiving, and those who preach the existence of the immaterial speak lying nonsense. When the body dies both fool and wise perish. They do not survive death."

Another sect was that of the Ajivakas, who believed in a destiny which individuals could not alter. Why practise austerities if you are bound to fate, one might ask? "Because," these fierce ascetics might have replied, "we are destined to asceticism." Some scholars have identified the pessimism noticeable in many of the non-orthodox philosophies with the uncertainties that are commonly associated with rapid social change and city life.

"Heroes and kings have given up their glory. The earth founders. The gods perish. I am," cried one man, "like a frog in a dry well."

Jains and Buddhists

A 13th-century illuminated leaf from the Kalpa Sutra, *a Jain manuscript detailing the lives of Jain saints and enumerating Jain monastic rules.*

One of the greatest of the new teachers was Mahavira (*c*.540–468BC), who founded Jainism (the religion of *jinas*, "conquerors"). Jainism, like Buddhism, has survived into the 20th century. But unlike the Buddhists, the Jains have always maintained a presence in India.

At the centre of Jainism is the notion that the soul – originally pure and blissful – is constantly subject to pollution through *karma*. Any action breeds *karma*, and the accumulation of *karma* leads to further birth; only by destroying *karma* can the soul become free and enter the eternal bliss that is the Jain *nirvana*. Mahavira attracted a large following of both monks and lay people, but *nirvana* could be attained only by those who followed the asceticism of monastic life.

The basis of Jain discipline lies in extreme non-violence. As souls reside in all phenomena, Jains must avoid hurting anything, living or inanimate. Like Buddhist monks, Jains strain their water to save small organisms. Unlike Buddhists, Jain monks veil their mouths so as not to inhale creatures, and carry whisks to brush insects from their tread. Without this perpetual, vigilant *ahimsa* (non-hurting), Jains would be plunged ever deeper into the misery of rebirth.

Mahavira, like the other new religious leaders and philosophers, rejected the Brahmanical notion of God or gods and the practice of rituals. All the new thinkers insisted on an ascetic style of life. All, except extreme materialists, believed in rebirth over vast cycles of time. While the Buddha himself proclaimed the doctrine of not-self or not-soul (*anatta*), the notion of rebirth remained central even to Buddhism. This created logical difficulties for later Buddhists – for how could there be rebirth if there was no soul to be reborn? Some Buddhist thinkers compare rebirth to a flame passing from one source to another without dying or changing identity: likewise in rebirth there is, with unfathomable ambiguity, just a "continuity of phenomena".

A Jain saint from Orissa, 11th century.

A Jain monk in the Adinath temple, Ranakpur, Rajasthan. Jains today follow the rituals and discipline set out by Mahavira in the 6th century BC. *This monk's mouth is covered so as not inadvertently to inhale tiny creatures.*

The beginnings of the religious community

An early 19-century Burmese palm-leaf manuscript of the Buddha's first sermon, the "Turning of the Wheel of Law". The circular decorations represent the wheel of dharma.

The Buddha's first sermon, known as the "Turning of the Wheel of Law", was addressed to the ascetics with whom he had formerly fasted. Expounding the Four Truths and the Middle Way, the Buddha concluded: "Thus, O monks, vision, knowledge and light arose. My mental release is now unshakeable. There is no rebirth." The five ascetics became the Buddha's first followers.

The Buddha's vision had become the doctrine. History and legend show the monastic order growing rapidly. Illustrating the way in which Buddhism penetrated the urban classes is the story of the rich merchant Yasa, who woke up one day to find his luxurious and sensual life stifling. He ran away from home to follow the Buddha, and his father pursued him. Both were soon converted, Yasa becoming the seventh member of the order and his father the first lay disciple. The first two women lay disciples were Yasa's mother and his wife. Fifty-four of Yasa's friends were ordained as monks. These sixty then left to spread the doctrine.

The Pali narratives (see p.71) emphasize how the Buddha drew followers both from secular society and from the disciples of other yogis. Among these yogis were two of the Buddha's most distinguished followers, Sariputra and Maudgalyayana. Sariputra became known as the greatest of the Buddha's preachers; Maudgalyayana was the "chief among those with magical powers" (*siddhis*). Other converts were two of the Buddha's cousins: Ananda, who would later become the Buddha's attendant, and Devadatta, who later tried to kill the Master (see p.49). The Buddha's son Rahula was ordained as a monk at the minimum age of twenty.

A 7th–8th-century wheel from Thailand represents the turning wheel of dharma.

In early days, before Buddhist rituals had evolved, to become a monk a man simply had to shave his head and beard, adopt yellow robes and recite the famous Triple Refuge. This simple formula is still used at the beginning of recitations, meditations and meals. Based on the "Triple Gem" of Buddha, *dharma* (doctrine), *sangha* (religious community), it is as follows:

I take refuge in the Buddha.
I take refuge in the dharma.
I take refuge in the sangha.

Although the Buddha had renounced excessive austerities, the monk's life was intensely disciplined. Later, more than 200 rules evolved for fully ordained *bhikkhus* (monks; literally "beggars"). The essence of the monastic code was, and is, contained in the "ten precepts":

To refrain from destroying living creatures; to refrain from taking that which is not given; to refrain from erotic behaviour; to refrain from incorrect speech; to refrain from liquors and drugs which lead to carelessness; to refrain from eating at the wrong times; to refrain from dancing, singing, music, going to shows, wearing garlands and beautifying oneself with perfumes and cosmetics; to refrain from lying on a high or luxurious sleeping place; to refrain from accepting money.

MONASTIC DISCIPLINE

Despite its discipline, the monk's life was seen as freer than a lay person's. In a discussion with King Ajatasattu the Buddha compares secular and monastic existence:

"The householder's life is full of hindrances. It is a dusty path … The homeless wanderer lives an uncluttered life. When a householder becomes a *bhikkhu*, he adopts principles of good bodily action and speech. He leads a wholesome life, observing the moral precepts; he is alert, contented and aware." The Buddha continues with an explanation of the Eightfold Path. This is his commentary on "right speech":

"Putting away lying words, the *bhikkhu* is aloof from falsehood. He speaks truth; faithful and trustworthy, he does not break his word to the world.

A young Theravada monk from Thailand inspects a Buddha figure's hand. Buddhist monks continue to follow the moral precepts laid down by the Buddha in the 6th century BC.

"Putting away slander, the *bhikkhu* is aloof from calumny. Thus he lives as a binder together of those who are divided, a speaker of words that make for peace.

"The *bhikkhu* is aloof from harsh language. Whatever word is blameless, lovely, moving, such are his words.

"The *bhikkhu* is aloof from vain conversation. He speaks at the appropriate time, in accordance with the facts, words full of meaning, on religion, on the discipline of the *sangha*. He speaks words worthy to be remembered, fitly illustrated, to the point."

Accounts of the Buddha's lifetime

It is impossible to piece together a realistic or chronological biography of the Buddha. Certainly the Buddha himself and many of his named followers and patrons existed. But all surviving texts concerning the Buddha's life were written hundreds of years after his death. It is not even known what language he spoke. Presumably in the kingdoms of Magadha and Kosala where he spent most of his life, the Buddha taught in the languages of those countries. It is unlikely that he spoke Sanskrit, the language of Indian classical literature and sacred Hindu texts. Pali, in which most of the early accounts of the Buddha's life were written, probably came into existence centuries after his death.

This 11th-century basalt statue from eastern India depicts the seated Buddha surrounded by scenes from his life.

Nevertheless, the Pali texts (see p.71), often give descriptions of a "Buddhist day" which are no doubt typical. The Buddha wakes early, meditates, takes his robe and bowl, walks with some of his community into a town for food offerings, returns to eat his meal, bathes, meditates, receives visitors and delivers a sermon. Meditating deep into the night, he then sleeps for a limited period before waking to repeat the same procedure.

Formulaic as such an account may be, it none the less provides us with a sense of the possible rhythm of the Master's life. Twentieth-century Buddhist monks still more or less follow this ancient routine.

However, sometimes the Pali texts do

INDIAN CULTURAL LIFE IN THE BUDDHA'S TIME

Highlighting the simplicity of the *bhikkhu*'s existence, one of the Pali texts gives a brilliant picture of cultural life, enumerating the worldly pleasures that are forbidden to Buddhists: ballad recitations, dances, drum-playing, acrobatics, elephant fights, boxing, wrestling, board and ball games and dice.

The opulence of material life is evoked in a list of couches, blankets, cosmetics and shampoos, which *bhikkhus* may not enjoy. Folk arts and occult activity such as fortune-telling, exorcism and the use of charms and amulets must also be avoided by Buddhists. To the monk who devotes his life to the *dharma*, all such interests are condemned as "low arts".

Women play games, dance and make music in this roundel from the Amaravati stupa.

A 19th-century Burmese manuscript illustration showing King Ajatasattu, usually represented with a beard, carrying one of the relics from the Buddha's parinirvana *(completed* nirvana*).*

give us intimate and lively details of particular moments, events or actions that were performed by the Buddha. In one text we read of him swimming in the Ganges; in another he approaches the meditation hall and waits for his followers to finish their conversation before coughing in order to announce his presence.

One famous text offers a particularly vivid picture, in which King Ajatasattu is visiting the Buddha at night. Frightened by the silence in the mango grove where the Master awaits him, the prince asks his tutor:

"How can it be that with twelve hundred and fifty *bhikkhus* surrounding him no voice can be heard, not a sneeze or a cough?"

"Move on, great raja," his tutor reassures him. "There's the round tent, and burning lights."

The prince goes forward, first on his elephant, then on foot, until he comes to the door of the great round tent. And the prince says to his tutor: "But where is the Master?"

"There he is, great raja. There is the Master, sitting by the middle tent-post, facing east, among his *bhikkhus*."

Buddhist meditation

The practice of meditation, if not universal, has probably always been widely dispersed. Tribal hunters awaiting game are, like Buddhist meditators, physically still and mentally concentrated. The shamans of these tribal societies likewise meditate in solitude in their quest for spirit visions. Even within the early Buddhist period, there was an enormous diversity of meditational practice. But all were intent on one thing: achieving release from *samsara*, the endless round of rebirths.

Like the sages of the Hindu *Upanishads* who strove to identify the personal soul with the world soul, the Buddhist sought the absolute. But because the Buddhist was not interested in phenomena lying beyond the individual, the Buddhist absolute was not absorption into a world spirit but the achievement of *nirvana*, an internal condition of ultimate not-self. The best way to attain this state is to become a monk, since this makes it easier to achieve moral perfection. For not only are the emotions of anger, hatred and sexual love themselves regarded as corruptions, but the life of emotion would muddle the process of meditation.

Recorded in a long narrative poem, *The Acts of the Buddha*, the Buddha's first meditation (see p.13) occurs on an outing to the forest with some court companions. The future Buddha's experience is easy and natural, arising spontaneously from three stimuli. The first is a longing for spiritual peace. The second is the Bodhisattva's compassionate reaction to the sight of exhausted ploughmen and oxen, and the tiny creatures killed by the ploughshare. The meditation arises thirdly from the Bodhisattva's sudden, pleasant separation from his companions, and his intense desire to achieve mental clarity.

A Thai Buddhist monk in temple grounds. Simply to stand is also to meditate.

A Buddhist nun meditating at a peace rally on the eve of the Cambodian elections, 1993.

Ploughmen in Bihar, India: fulfilling their role in society – or suffering and causing suffering?

This experience occurred before he left his father's court. When, after his renunciation of the luxuries of his former life, the homeless Bodhisattva subsequently went for training with meditation masters, he was quickly able to attain states of consciousness which represented his teachers' highest experience. Dissatisfied with this level of insight, the future Buddha went on to achieve his enlightenment alone.

THE *JHANAS* (LEVELS OF ABSORPTION)

The Buddha was to build some of the techniques that he learned from his meditation teachers into his own *jhana* (absorption) meditational process. This is the process which is defined in the Eightfold Path (see pp.25–7) as *samadhi* (meditative concentration).

The *jhanas* are described in the following stages. The first *jhana* is accompanied by thought and is filled with rapture and joy. In the second *jhana* tranquillity, oneness of mind and rapture replace thought. The third *jhana* is a state of equanimity and awareness. In the fourth *jhana* all pleasure and pain are obliterated by equanimity and mental one-pointedness.

The fifth *jhana* dwells beyond perception of matter in boundless space. In the sixth *jhana* the mind reaches boundless consciousness. Beyond consciousness in the seventh *jhana*, the mind dwells in the sphere of nothingness. Beyond the sphere of nothingness is neither-perception-nor-non-perception, which is the eighth and last *jhana*.

A young Theravada monk at his ordination in Cambodia. His elderly relative wears the white of the lay devotee. Meditative concentration will form a part of the monk's training.

A Sri Lankan temple in the process of construction, dominated by a colossal meditating Buddha.

The most famous discourse on meditation is the *Satipatthana (*Foundations of Awareness) *Sutra.* While the first stages of *jhana* meditation (see p.45) flow from the practice of "right concentration" as prescribed by the Eightfold Path (see pp.26), so awareness meditation is practice in the "right awareness" of the Eightfold Path. And while concentration functions partly for the achievement of tranquillity (*samatha*), the awareness that arises once tranquillity has been achieved may lead the meditator to complete enlightenment.

In this *Sutra*, the Buddha analyzes four "foundations of awareness". To achieve complete awareness, the practitioner must focus on the five components (*skandhas*; see p.29) of a human being, that is, the body, feeling, consciousness, perception and mental formations with their karmic deposits. The Master describes the conditions and environment conducive to meditation. The *bhikkhu* (monk) must go to the forest, to the foot of a tree or to an empty place. He sits cross-legged with his body straight, and arouses awareness of his breathing: "Aware, he breathes in; aware, he breathes out. Thinking, 'I breathe in long', he understands that he breathes in long. So on through inspirations and expirations, long and short. 'Experiencing the whole body, calming the activity of the body, I shall breathe in.' So he trains himself."

In watching the breath, the practitioner is meditating on the life and movement of the body. This is no different from the concentration that goes into an overtly non-meditational process: "Just as an intelligent turner of wood who turns a long turn understands 'I turn long', or when he turns short understands 'I turn short', so it is with the contemplation of the breath. Thus he lives contemplating the body within the body, and contemplates the origination of phenomena in the body and the dissolution of phenomena in the body. Or his awareness is established with the thought: 'There is a body.' Thus he lives independently and clings to nothing in the world."

The exercise is repeated with respect to feelings, consciousness, perceptions and mental objects. Awareness meditation may be practised in the postures of sitting, lying, standing and walking. Such heightened moment-to-moment attention extends to all ordinary details of life: chewing, tasting, swallowing, urinating, defecating. By this process of self-observation, meditators come to know their life past and present, and to understand its perpetual changes.

The rise and fall of the breath is often interpreted as a sign for birth and death. By watching the breath, a practitioner develops a deeper consciousness of the "rising and falling away" process which is the mark of all life. Rather than develop "self-knowledge", awareness meditation seeks to comprehend life as a changing series of impersonal processes in which ego dissolves within the flux of phenomena. Indifferent in their equanimity to joy or pain, practitioners then see things as they are – filled with suffering, impermanent, without self – as the Buddha described them. When this abstraction becomes an experience, phenomena which had been "out there" or within individual consciousness simply become what is.

A young monk with his family at a Buddhist temple in Kathmandu, Nepal.

BODY AND CEMETERY MEDITATION

Meditation on the body is predicated on two descriptions of its character. First, the body is composed of four elements (*dhatu*): earth, water, fire and wind: the earth element provides the body's solidity, animated and supported by the three mobile *dhatus*. The practitioner is further enjoined to contemplate thirty-two parts of the body. There is no intrinsic virtue in a knowledge of the body's structure: the purpose of the discipline is to reduce the meditator's delusory sense of "self" to a vision of personhood that is impermanent (*anicca*) and without self (*anatta*).

Another aspect of awareness meditation is meditation on death. Just as *bhikkhus* contemplate their living, changing bodies, so they must meditate on corpses. "And further," says the Buddha, "if a *bhikkhu* sees a dead body thrown into a charnel ground, he thinks of his own body thus: 'Truly, my own body is of the same nature as that body. It will be like that body. It has not got past the condition of becoming like that body.'" Only through a fearless comprehension of mortality will the meditator arrive at a clear view of reality.

The Buddha and the supernatural

The sublimity of the Buddha's teaching is strangely accompanied by fragmentary and anecdotal legends about the circumstances both of his past lives and of his historical life. Some of these stories – such as the legends of generosity in the birth tales (see pp.22–3) – convey a wisdom or morality which harmonizes with the Buddha's teaching. But while in many accounts of the Buddha's life we can feel the dust of ancient India underfoot, other stories deal with supernatural events which belong firmly to the realm of folklore.

Like the majority of people of his time, the Buddha saw no reason not to believe in non-empirical reality. He spoke frequently of deities, spirits, heaven and hell; and although he seems to have regarded the supernatural realm as relatively unimportant, he also seems to have taken its existence for granted.

There are, in this connection, a number of stories attributing supernatural powers to the Buddha. And although the Master for the most part discouraged his followers from practising the occult arts, it was generally believed that certain levels of meditative concentration resulted in magical powers, such as were achieved by yogic adepts. Some senior *bhikkhus*, like the Buddha himself, are attributed with magical or shamanistic prowess.

LEGENDS OF THE SUPERNATURAL

The most dramatic accounts of the Master's feats read like legends of mythical heroes and deities such as Krishna in human incarnation. Among other feats, the Buddha overcame great snakes (*nagas*) which vomited smoke and flame, read thoughts, received visits from the gods, and flew to the Heaven of the Thirty-three Gods to teach the mothers of previous Buddhas. His most celebrated legendary exploits were the Miracle of the Rose-apple Tree and the Miracle of the Pairs.

In the first of these, the young Bodhisattva sat for many hours under a rose-apple tree – whose protective shadow never moved.

The second miracle took place after King Suddhodana invited his son – now the Buddha – to visit his court. The Master arrived, with 20,000 *arhats* (enlightened people), but when some of his kinsmen refused to acknowledge him, "the Buddha rose in the air, flames came from the upper part of his body and streams of water from the lower part. Then the process was reversed. Next, fire came from the right side of his body and water from the left, and so on through twenty-two variations of pairs. Then he created a jewelled promenade in the sky, and walking along it produced the illusion that he was standing or sitting or lying down."

A panel from the east gate of the Sanchi stupa *(1st century AD), illustrating one of the miracles by which the Buddha converted Kashyapa, who became a major disciple.*

Many people find it hard to reconcile such mythopoetic elements in the Buddha's story with the rational, non-deistic nature of his ethical teachings. But the ancient mind was clearly capable of simultaneously incorporating both the empirical and supernatural dimensions. The combination of both realms in the Buddha *dharma* is richly textured and metaphorically alive in ways that have become strange to modern consciousness.

Theravada tradition has it that the Buddha displayed his supernatural powers following victorious debates with "heretics". In this Burmese manuscript from c.*1840, the Buddha is shown emanating fire, and in the right-hand panel, ascending to heaven.*

DEVADATTA ATTEMPTS TO KILL THE BUDDHA

Devadatta, a cousin of the Buddha who had joined the *sangha* (monastic community), tried late in the Master's life to take over the leadership of the community. When his bid was rejected, Devadatta – with the assent of the parricide King Ajatasattu – plotted to kill the Buddha. The story suggests tensions within both the *sangha* and the kingdom of Magadha, but its other main interest lies in its supernatural content.

In one murder attempt, Devadatta hurled a rock at the Buddha from the Vulture Peak, where the Buddha had frequently preached. "But two peaks came together and crushed the rock. Only a falling splinter made the Master's foot bleed." On another occasion, Devadatta set loose a man-killing elephant on the Buddha. "But the Master pervaded the elephant with loving-kindness. Taking dust from the Master's feet and sprinkling his own head, the elephant retired bowing." Devadatta eventually sank into hell.

A 2nd–3rd-century AD *carved relief from Gandhara (Pakistan/Afghanistan), showing an attempt to murder the Buddha by Devadatta's men, who are now stricken with remorse (left).*

Naive though these stories may appear, the mountain incident illustrates how the environment of the Buddha "vibrated sympathetically" with the Buddha's *dharma*. The elephant story exemplifies the healing power of loving-kindness (*metta*).

The last days of the Buddha

The Buddha's last days are described in the long Pali text called the *Great Parinirvana Sutra* (*parinirvana* meaning "completed *nirvana*"). The Buddha's living *nirvana*, achieved during enlightenment, at death transforms to *nirvana* without human residue. The *Sutra* shows the Buddha on his final journey, in 486BC and with vivid realism takes us through the region where he had taught for forty-five years. Three main strands – personal, doctrinal and historical – inform this vital scripture.

In the personal sphere, we see the Buddha weary and sick, needing rest under shady trees and aware that death approaches. In a series of conversations between the Master and his attendant, Ananda, the Buddha's equanimity contrasts powerfully with Ananda's straightforward misery. After one bout of sickness, Ananda exclaims, "At the sight of your illness, my body became weak, the horizon grew unclear, my senses reeled."

The Buddha rebukes him for wanting too much: "What does the *sangha* [community] expect, Ananda? I have given you the doctrine. I am not like those teachers with one fist closed on [hiding] esoteric teaching." This remark may represent a Hinayana writer's response to a Mahayanist claim that the Buddha kept back the "secret wisdom" later revealed by the Mahayana (see p.64). The Buddha continues with this startling image: "I am eighty. My body is like an old cart held together with straps. Only when I am deep in meditation is my body comfortable."

The doctrinal and historical converge in the Buddha's directions for the future. To strengthen the *sangha*'s confidence, the Buddha reviews his teaching on

This colossal 12th-century recumbent Buddha in Polonnaruwa, Sri Lanka, is part of an ensemble of four large figures, and depicts the Buddha in death or parinirvana.

THE DEATH OF THE BUDDHA

Self-possessed, without psychological pain, untroubled by the thought of death, the Buddha identifies four places of future pilgrimage: the sites of his birth, enlightenment, first sermon, and death. "But don't hinder yourselves by honouring my remains," he adds.

Ananda continues grieving. With his head bent against a door-frame, "I am just a beginner!" he bitterly cries. "Don't grieve, Ananda!" the Buddha consoles him. "The nature of things dictates that we must leave those dear to us. Everything born contains its own cessation." He then praises Ananda's devotion: "With effort, Ananda, you will attain *nirvana*."

They reach Kushinara, "a small wattle-and-daub jungle town", as Ananda exclaims, "unfit for a Buddha's *parinirvana*." Unconcerned, the Master invites the *sangha* to confess any doubts they might have in the *dharma*. The *bhikkhus* stand silent. "Not one, Ananda, has misgivings. All will eventually reach enlightenment." The Buddha then utters his final words, "Listen, *bhikkhus*, I say this: all conditioned things are subject to decay. Strive with diligence."

ethics, meditation and wisdom, and sums up the *dharma* in thirty-seven points, including the Eightfold Path, the Foundations of Awareness and the Seven Factors of Enlightenment. "So long as monks meet as a unified group, maintain the *sangha*'s rules and train themselves in self-possession, it will prosper," promises the Master. But: "Be your own lamps. Be your own refuge. Hold fast to the *dharma*," he enjoins them. "Do not look for refuge beyond yourselves. This way you will overcome darkness."

Then the Buddha walks with Ananda to some trees outside the town of Vesali. "How lovely this spot is with its tree shrines, Ananda!" he exclaims. He then implies that he might, at another's request, preternaturally extend his life; when Ananda overlooks the remark, the Buddha expresses irritation.

How this episode harmonizes with the Buddha's acceptance of death is not clear. Certainly the Master is ready for death at the time of his last meal. This is the gift of the metal-smith Chunda, who has prepared a dish for the *sangha*. Perceiving danger in the meat, the Buddha orders Chunda to serve it to him alone and bury the rest. Soon the Buddha is stricken with fatal dysentery. But he insists that Chunda should feel no remorse, for one who donates a Buddha's last meal acquires great merit.

Early Indian and Mahayana Buddhism

In the 500 years after the Buddha's death, about twenty monastic schools emerged in India, some separated by differing codes of conduct, some by distance. Around the 1st century AD a new religious climate arose. Dissatisfaction with monkish elitism, intense philosophical speculation, and the influence of Hindu devotionalism led to the formation of the Mahayana (Great Vehicle) – virtually a new Buddhist religion. Despite disputes between Mahayanist and Hinayanist (Small Vehicle) rivals, these groups often lived amicably within the same monasteries.

There were two main tendencies in Indian Mahayana, one devotional, the other philosophical. As devotional Buddhism drew closer to Hinduism, part of its original character was absorbed. Later, the Islamic conquest pushed Buddhism further into obscurity until by the 15th century it had vanished from Indian soil. The 20th century has seen a small revival. Aided by the Indian Mahabodhi Society, ancient sites have been reclaimed, and new temples built. Also, a significant population of Hindu *harijans* (formerly "untouchables") on the west coast followed the politician B.R. Ambedkhar by converting to Buddhism in the late 1940s. These communities are now well established.

The face of a gilded statue of the bodhisattva *Maitreya (the Buddha of the future) in the Tikse monastery, Ladakh. The* bodhisattva *figure represents a major element in Mahayana thought. Maitreya will manifest himself as a Buddha in the far distant future: but only after Buddhist doctrine has been forgotten.*

After the Buddha's *parinirvana*

A week after the Buddha's death in Kushinara, his body was taken to the east of the village. There, wrapped in cotton and placed in an iron vessel, the body was cremated on a perfumed funeral pyre. The news of the Buddha's death spread through the countries of the Ganges valley, and state messengers arrived quickly to claim relics for their masters. As though to suggest that the Buddha had, himself, burned away his grosser elements, his body is said to have left no ashes. The remaining bones were divided between eight places. A monumental *stupa* (reliquary) was built to mark each burial, "eight *stupas* for the remains, one for the cremation vessel and one for the wood embers".

The following rainy season a convocation of *bhikkhus* assembled in the monastery at Rajagaha for the first Buddhist Council. The community was headed by Kassapa (Kashyapa) the Great, who chose 499 *arhats* (those of perfect enlightenment) to compose the Council. The purpose of this meeting was to establish a canon of the Buddha *dharma*. To this end, the *bhikkhu* Upali recited the rules of the monastic discipline (*Vinaya*) along with details of how each rule had come into being. Then Ananda, who had lived at the Buddha's side as his attendant, was called on to recite the Master's discourses (*sutras*). Ananda had not achieved enlightenment, but before his recital, he succeeded through meditation in arriving at the inner freedom of an *arhat*.

The *Sutras* and the *Vinaya* constitute two of the great bodies (*pitaka*, literally "basket") of the Buddha's teaching that have been preserved. The third *pitaka*, a formidable body of texts called the *Abhidharma* (Analysis of, or Further *Dharma*) was probably composed later. Although writing at this time was used for business and administration, the Buddha's teachings were not yet written down. Instead, groups of monks memorized particular traditions within the canon, and in this way they preserved the *dharma*.

THE *ARHAT*

During the Buddha's last illness, Ananda is painfully aware that he has not achieved enlightenment or become an *arhat* (enlightened person). The term applied to those who had rid themselves of self or any notion of "mine" and were without craving, hatred and delusion. An *arhat*, like the Buddha, would not suffer rebirth. Later, Buddhists described stages on the path to *arhat*ship: "stream winners", who had entered the stream to *nirvana*; "once-returners", who would have one more birth; "non-returners", who would be born again only among gods before entering *nirvana*.

An 18th-century depiction of an arhat; *a golden complexion is a sign of advanced spirituality.*

THE *STUPA*

The domed shape of the Buddhist *stupa* or pagoda may have derived from ancient mounds which marked the burials of tribal dignitaries. The ten *stupas* built over the remains of the Buddha were soon followed by similar monuments that consecrated the relics of monks and ritual objects. *Stupas* were generally donated by lay people, and were used as objects of meditation for pilgrims.

The symbolism of the *stupa* is varied and complex. A spire on the top of the dome suggests the Buddha's compassion. The dome itself represents *nirvana*, the absolute. The square base of the dome symbolizes moral restraint. Buried below the *stupa* base lies a receptacle for relics, a fragment of a monk's belongings, or a Buddhist inscription.

Some excavated *stupas* reveal domes densely carved with Buddhist symbols and scenes from the Buddha's life. In the example above right, panels depict the First Sermon and *Jataka* stories (see pp.22–3); garlands and symbolic "three jewels" decorate the upper dome; worshipping deities fill the outer margins. Guardian lions and elephants symbolize the Buddha's royal status. Many *stupas* are surrounded by decorated railings. Pilgrims walk and bow in a clockwise direction around the *stupa* meditating on the scenes depicted.

A carving on the drum of the great Amaravati stupa. *The seated Buddha (lower centre) holds his hand in the fear-allaying gesture.*

The Ruwanweli Dagaba at Anuradhapura. Possibly established in the time of the Singhalese king Duttha Gamani (101–77 BC), this heavily restored stupa *is one of the largest ever built. Like the Indian emperor Ashoka (see pp.58–9) in the 3rd century BC, King Gamani tried to expiate massive wartime slaughter by propagating Buddhism. According to the* Mahavamsa, *the chronicle of early Sri Lankan history, the central chamber of the otherwise solid dome contains a jewelled* bodhi *(enlightenment) tree made of precious metals.*

Buddhism in society

The essential aims of the Buddha were twofold: to arrive at an understanding of the truth which would lead from rebirth to *nirvana*; and to teach this truth and establish a society of monks and lay people who could follow his example. The newly enlightened Buddha had originally thought that his enlightenment experience was too subtle to be communicated. He was, nevertheless, soon convinced that there were people with sufficient intelligence to understand his teaching.

To understand and follow the Buddhist path fully it was necessary to become a monk. This meant abandoning society and living, to some extent, cut off from ordinary life. The words "cutting off", "leaving" and "withdrawal" recur frequently in Buddhist texts. Monks shave their hair and beards – thus symbolically cutting off sexual and familial attachments. Then, they "go forth" from society into a state of homelessness. Finally, they seek lonely places in which to meditate.

Some early Buddhist teaching suggests that it is only monks who may attain nirvana. *These lay devotees in Thailand are seeking help from the Buddha in* nirvana.

Despite this process of withdrawal, early Buddhism was a social force. The Buddha spent much of his life in the towns of northeast India, mixed with people from all ranks, and had much to say on the nature of social responsibility. At the heart of the Buddha's social thought was his view that people were essentially of common origin and should care for each other equally. "May all beings be happy," reads one famous text; another reads, "The monk pervades the whole world with a mind filled with friendliness and compassion, free from hatred and malevolence."

Women in Bangkok conducting puja *(worship) in a Buddhist temple with incense and chanting.*

In the Brahmanical system there were four castes: *brahmin* (priestly caste), *kshatriya* (warrior caste), *vaishya* (merchant caste) and *shudra* (worker or servant caste). The *brahmins* justified their high status by claiming that they were "born from the the mouth of the god Brahma". Opposing this idea, a Buddhist legend describes how people were originally "beings" who were "made of

Offerings of food signify generosity and contribute to the devotee's store of merit that leads to favourable rebirth.

LAY DISCIPLES

As monastic society grew, so did the Buddhist lay community. The monks were dependent on lay people both for their daily meal and for other necessities, including robe-material, razors, bowls and shelter during the rainy season. With a few exceptions, it was assumed that lay followers neither sought nor achieved *nirvana*. Instead they were promised favourable rebirth on earth or in one of the heavens.

When Anathapindada, one of the Buddha's most famous lay supporters, was dying, two monks arrived to teach him meditation and non-attachment. Hearing their discourse, the sick man wept. He had never been offered the higher doctrine.

Like many others, Anathapindada had been given instruction only in the five precepts against killing, stealing, verbal and sexual misconduct and the use of intoxicants. He was reborn into the (somewhat undistinguished) realm of the gods. Lay people in many Buddhist countries today are often, similarly, taught an ethical Buddhism. Working people have little time to meditate. But if they follow the five precepts and practise generosity, they will accumulate the "merit" that leads to ever better births.

mind". Beautiful, disembodied and self-luminous, these beings lived, feeding on joy, until one of them, a trickster, picked up some deliciously edible earth which had formed on the water. Other beings copied the trickster. As they ate, they lost their luminosity. The degeneration continued. The beings acquired bodies, then property and sexuality. Theft, punishment and government evolved. The new people finally established an aristocracy and a priesthood. But despite caste differences, everyone had common origin in the "beings".

Thus, even if people, as the Buddha suggested, "had dust in their eyes", this was on account of their personal *karma*, not of their social status.

The regulation of the monastic community was based on mutual respect and discussion. Certainly, there were senior monks and novices, but all followed the same rule, and the Buddha appointed no successor to himself. The organization of the community was modelled less on monarchy than on a republic such as Vajji. The Buddha, none the less, stressed that where monarchy existed, the king should follow the five precepts (see above), and should provide the means for his subjects to live in prosperity. The emperor Ashoka attempted, uniquely, to rule almost the entire subcontinent according to the Buddhist *dharma* (see pp.58–9).

The emperor Ashoka

An Ashokan pillar edict from Sarnath (3rd century BC), with a warning of expulsion to dissident monks.

Two centuries after the Buddha's death, the north-eastern kingdom of Magadha (see map on p.34), where the Buddha had spent much of his life, had become an empire extending to the far west and to southern India. Between 268 and 239BC this empire was ruled by a remarkable emperor who became a Buddhist layman. This was the celebrated Ashoka, who was known as "the Just", on account both of his piety and of his mission to spread Buddhism. The emperor had previously given most of his support to the Ajivaka sect (see p.37) and, like most Indian kings, he continued to practise religious toleration. But after he became a lay Buddhist around 260BC, Ashoka attempted to rule by *dharma*: the justice, non-violence and generosity associated with Buddhist teaching.

The emperor had the usual means of administration at his disposal: an army, revenue collectors, civil servants and ambassadors. But Ashoka's fame rests on the inscribed edicts that he distributed on rocks and pillars throughout his empire.

By his own admission, Ashoka had not always been pious. Following a war of conquest in eastern India, the emperor experienced a crisis of conscience. In the most famous of his "rock edicts" in 265BC, he publicly proclaimed remorse for the victims of his war of conquest. "When the beloved of the gods [Ashoka] had been king for eight years, he conquered Kalinga: 150,000 people were carried off to slavery; 100,000 were killed. Many times that number died of other causes. Now Ashoka is intensely concerned with justice and the *dharma*. Ashoka grieves over his conquest. The thought of conquest, death and slavery is strongly felt, a heavy thought in the emperor. The common humanity of all people is a heavy thought for the emperor." He then proclaims his intention to refrain from future violence and hopes that his descendants will do likewise.

Ashoka was an ethical Buddhist, and his edicts provide no evidence of any philosophical interest. But his ethics were sincere, and although his empire began its decline soon after his death, Ashoka's attempt to rule by *dharma* was unique. His drive toward unity within his realms did not rule out tolerance. "One should honour another man's sect ... concord is to be commended so that men may hear one another's principles," says one edict.

Ashoka promoted justice too: "In the past there were no high officials for justice," he declared. "They have been created by me thirteen years after my consecration, among servants and masters, the *brahmins* and the wealthy, the poor, old people, for benefit and happiness." In a pillar edict late in his reign, he also proclaimed that he had "banyan trees planted for shade to beasts and men ... mango groves planted, and ... wells dug and rest houses built every nine miles [14km]."

The Buddha had recommended that kings should be protective and generous. Ashoka conformed to that injunction. "I have done these things," he said, "in order that my people might conform to the *dharma*."

The best preserved of Ashokan columns, dating from 243 BC, carved from polished sandstone and engraved with seven imperial edicts at Lauryiya Nandangarh, Nepal.

THE FOUR-LION CAPITAL

Most of Ashoka's inscriptions are in dialects of the Prakrit languages spoken in northern India. But in the far western regions (modern Pakistan and Afghanistan), there are inscriptions in Greek for the descendants of Alexander the Great's armies and in the semitic language of Aramaic for those familiar with the language of the Persian empire. The most famous of Ashoka's columns has a four-lion capital (see left). The lion symbolizes both Ashoka's imperial rule and the kingship of the Buddha. The four-lion capital was adopted as the emblem of the modern Indian republic.

The growth of Mahayana

Around 500 years after the death of the Buddha, in the 1st and 2nd centuries AD, a major revolution in Buddhist thought took place. The movement arose out of ideas that had been evolving over a long period in a number of sects in southern and northwestern India. The new Buddhist thinkers called their system Mahayana, the "great vehicle" or "ferryboat", and they sometimes described the older Buddhist schools, pejoratively, as the Hinayana, the "little ferryboat".

Mahayana thought developed partly as a response to demands of Indian lay Buddhists. Buddhism up to this point had been largely the preserve of monks. Lay people were excluded from full participation in religious activity, and the monkish *arhat* (enlightened person) came increasingly to be regarded as a spiritual aristocrat on the path to a purely personal salvation. The doctrine of "not-self" (see pp.28–9) made little public sense if the practitioner seemed to be using it for self-benefit. According to Buddhist thought, no one could truly become an *arhat* if they had not, with insight and compassion, burned the notion of self away. None the less, 500 years of monastic endeavour seemed to have left Buddhist culture somewhat weary, and true *arhats* were hard to identify.

The new Mahayana constituency made its appeal to both monks and lay people – the importance of the laity being illustrated in the person of Vimalakirti, a character from Sanskrit fiction whose insight and compassion matched his involvement in civic life.

Central to "great vehicle" idealism was a shift of focus from *arhat* to *bodhisattva* (enlightenment being). In earlier Buddhism, *bodhisattva* denoted a previous incarnation of the Buddha. The term was taken up by Mahayanists in its literal sense: a person made of, or for, enlightenment. *Bodhisattvas* were those who vowed they would be enlightened. But this enlightenment was not for themselves alone: it was pursued for the salvation of others. The *bodhisattvas'* vow went further: they would refuse entry into *nirvana* until they had led all other beings there before them.

The high altruism of such a position had its results in the realm of faith and belief. For to achieve their aim, *bodhisattvas* would suffer rebirth over countless aeons, millions of times. But an ordinary mortal could make the vow: and this brought universal compassion to the centre of Buddhist practice.

THE SYMBOLS OF THE FLOOD AND FERRY

The Mahayana image of the "great ferryboat" developed a symbol that is general to Indian religions. Hindu and Jain as well as Buddhist thought conceives of suffering and rebirth (*samsara*) as an ocean or river-flood which separates humanity from *nirvana* (enlightenment). Jain saviours, for example, are called "crossing-makers". In one of the Buddha's famous discourses, the *dharma* (doctrine) is compared to a makeshift raft.

"Certainly," said the Buddha, "my teaching will take you across the flood. But once on the other shore, who has need of the raft itself? The raft is for crossing, not for hanging on to."

This teaching of non-attachment to Buddhist doctrine was further developed by Mahayana philosophers.

The river Ganges at dawn. Particularly when flooded, the Ganges furnished Indian Buddhists with a symbol of the endlessness of samsara *(the cycle of rebirth). Mahayana teachers claimed that their doctrines represented a "great ferryboat" for delivering humanity to the "other shore" of* nirvana *(enlightenment). Mahayanists accused their Hinayana opponents of providing only a small vessel with which a spiritual elite could make the crossing.*

Bodhisattvas, in Mahayana thought, might be perfected human beings or mythologized figures such as Avalokiteshvara, or Maitreya, the future Buddha who was believed to be already at work in history for the welfare of all beings. Another major mythologizing component in Mahayana was the transformation of the Buddha himself into a transcendental god-like figure.

The *bodhisattva* is an adept of the "six perfections" (*paramitas*) of generosity, patience, meditation, morality, energy and wisdom. The most significant of these is generosity. When Avalokiteshvara (Chinese Kuan-Yin, see p.93; Japanese Kannon) was about to enter *nirvana*, there was an uproar of grief in the universe. In a supreme act of generosity, the *bodhisattva* drew back so as to continue his work as guardian and saviour.

A gilt bronze figure of a bodhisattva, *possibly the future Buddha Maitreya, from 19th-century Nepal.*

In the Pali texts (see p.71), the Buddha was depicted as a man – the prince Siddhartha Gautama – whose departure into *nirvana* left the world without a Buddha. The Mahayana thinkers questioned whether a Buddha would quite simply have gone out of existence in the same way as the *arhats* whom they criticized for focusing on their own personal salvation. Consequently, there arose the doctrine of the Buddha's Triple Body (*Tri-kaya*). This doctrine asserts that in ultimate reality, and as an equivalent of *nirvana*, there is the Buddha's *dharma-kaya* (body of essence): this is the absolute which underlies all phenomena. Emanating from the *dharma-kaya*, and living as supreme

YOGACARA: SCHOOL OF "MIND ONLY"

The ideas of the Madhyamika school, perfected by Nagarjuna (see p.64), were extended some time later by two innovators from Gandhara, the half-brothers Asanga and Vasubandhu. They established the school of Yogacara, which proposed that phenomena were a creation of the individual mind, although a universal "store consciousness" (*alaya vijnana*) made shared experience possible. *Nirvana* was achieved when "pure thought" without falsifying objects of thought was sustained.

Yogacara also posits an absolute called "suchness" (*tathata*). This is an inexpressible condition equal to Madhyamika "emptiness" (*shunyata*). But the equivalence of *shunyata* and *nirvana* underpin both these Mahayana systems.

A major Yogacara book which elaborates both *tathata* and *shunyata* is the *Lankavatara Sutra* (5th century AD). This is said to have been the chosen text of Bodhidharma, the south Indian missionary to China (see pp.94–5). Chinese Ch'an ideas derive in part from Bodhidharma's reading of this *Sutra*, and both Ch'an and Zen are developments of the Yogacara system (see pp.94–7 and pp.112–19 respectively).

deity in heaven, is the Buddha's *sambhoga-kaya* (body of bliss). From the body of bliss emerges the Buddha's *nirmana-kaya* (body of magical transformation) – the human and yet suprahuman Buddha of northeast Indian history.

This complex, transcendental system is a radical departure from the more humanistic teachings recorded in the Pali texts. Clearly there are influences, in this aspect of Mahayana, from popular Hindu devotional cults (*bhakti*), and Persian and Greco-Roman theologies which filtered into India from the northwest.

But a corollary to this new theology, which offered salvation in a Buddha heaven, was democratically down-to-earth. The Mahayana devotee might pay homage to or even worship the Buddha deity: but that was on the understanding that all beings had Buddha nature. The worshipper and his or her object of devotion were ultimately the same. On another level of practice, it was the meditator's work to recognize the Buddha as himself or herself (a practice taken up later by Ch'an Buddhism; see pp.94–7).

While devotional Mahayana took Buddhism closer to the realm of a deistic religion, Mahayana philosophers led the system in the opposite direction. The basis of their philosophical thrust was a modulation of the earlier not-self (*anatta*) doctrine (see pp.28–9). This, in Hinayana, postulates that all phenomena are transitory and without essential character.

This 8th- to 9th-century bronze statue from Betong, Thailand, depicts Avalokiteshvara, the bodhisattva *who epitomized compassion*

The most influential of the new Mahayana schools was the Madhyamika (Those who Hold the Middle View), which extended this position to suggest that the voidness or emptiness of phenomena (*shunyata*) represents an absolute that is *nirvana* itself. This absolute – equivalent to the *dharma-kaya* of the Buddha's "three bodies" – is impossible to describe or conceive; it is the realm of enlightenment; here, beyond and without change; emptiness eternal.

To these Mahayana thinkers, all devotional symbols such as the *bodhisattva*, heaven and the three bodies of the Buddha are fictions. Such images are useful, firstly in that they offer devotees an experience of sublime mystification; secondly, because they point beyond the unsayable. But, argue the philosphers, metaphor and devotion themselves are an illusory stage furniture. Furthermore, the whole *dharma*, the notion of enlightenment, even the Buddha himself, are simply intellectual constructs whose value is metaphorical: they point to transcendent reality. Total reality has nothing to do with anything that can be named. Only emptiness exists, and even to say this is to mask reality from the intuitive, silent meditational experience in which it may be non-verbally, non-conceptually apprehended.

The perfection of wisdom

A vast outpouring of creative thought accompanied the development of Mahayana. The larger monasteries, to which monks travelled for instruction from specialist teachers, built libraries of every kind of Indian religious literature. Nalanda university in Bihar was described by Chinese pilgrims in the 5th century AD as having students, lecture series and Buddhist philosophical training in great abundance.

The remains of a 6th-century temple at the monastic university at Nalanda (5th–13th centuries), India's most celebrated centre of Mahayana scholarship, in Bihar, eastern India.

Mahayanists claimed that the new Mahayana texts contained the words of the Buddha himself, and that the Master had hidden his most important discoveries for some 500 years in the protective infernal realms of *nagas* (serpent or dragon kings). This view partly explains the name of the great Madhyamika philosopher Nagarjuna (Arjuna of the Nagas), a resident of Nalanda whom legend claimed to have been a *naga*. The Mahayana writers expounded their visions of the new philosophies in imaginary dialogues between *bodhisattvas* or between the Buddha and a disciple in some mythological site such as the "palace of the Sea-Serpents" or the "castle of Lanka on the peak of Mount Malaya".

A Tibetan visualization of the naga *(serpent) king Varuna seated on a lotus lifted by serpents, with a rain-giving deity in the background. The mystical landscape conflates infernal, worldly and celestial realms.*

One important group of texts, the *Prajnaparamita*, expounds the "perfection of wisdom". Besides generosity, it is wisdom, penetrating insight into the nature of existence, that characterizes the *bodhisattva* (enlightenment being). The *Heart Sutra*, so called because it sums up the essence or heart of Mahayana Buddhism, opens as follows: "The *bodhisattva* Avalokiteshvara was moving in the deep course of the perfection of wisdom [or the wisdom that

A painted 13th-century Prajnaparamita *book-cover depicting "perfect wisdom" as a deity. The goddess Prajnaparamita's two central hands converge in the teaching or discussion gesture; her top right hand holds a* vajra, *symbol of absolute reality; her top left hand holds the* Prajnaparamita *(Perfect Wisdom) text that she personifies. She is surrounded by symbolically coloured* bodhisattvas *and Taras* (female saviours).

PERFECT WISDOM AS A DEITY

Paradoxically, the refined nature of Mahayana wisdom was personified in a goddess, Prajnaparamita (Perfection of Wisdom). In the *Sutra of 8,000 Verses* the deity is praised as follows: "She is worthy of worship. In her we find refuge. She brings us safely under the wings of enlightenment. She is omniscience. Emptiness is her characteristic. She is the mother of the *bodhisattvas*. She is the perfect wisdom of the Buddhas. She turns the wheel of the *dharma*."

The goddess, like a Hindu deity, is sometimes depicted with four arms to suggest her many attributes. Her hands are shown in ritual positions (*mudras*) in the teaching, discussion and fear-allaying gestures. The lotus, as a symbol of purity and perfection, is her emblem.

has gone beyond]. He looked down from on high and saw just five heaps [the human personality; see p.29]. And he saw that in their own-being they were empty." The text goes on to explore the "emptiness of all phenomena"; speaking in a nameless mythological realm to the Buddha's disciple Sariputra, the *bodhisattva* says: "Here, O Sariputra, form [or matter] is emptiness, and emptiness is form. Whatever is emptiness, that is form: the same is true of the other constituents of personality."

Then, in an astonishing flight of paradoxical negation, he incorporates the whole of the Buddha's teaching into the vision of emptiness. The Buddha had taught that suffering and rebirth stem directly from ignorance. The mythical *bodhisattva* now claimed: "There is no ignorance, no elimination of ignorance; no suffering; no Eightfold Path; no attainment of enlightenment, and no non-attainment."

The "perfection of wisdom" refers to *nirvana* on the other side of the ocean of *samsara*. Mahayana writers extended their paradoxical negations further. Once arrived on the other shore the spiritual traveller would find it identical with "this shore". *Nirvana* is not over there. It is here in *samsara*. "Gone! Gone! Gone beyond! Gone altogether beyond!" concludes the *Heart Sutra*. But that "beyond" is neither in the *bodhisattva*'s myth realm nor in some distant aeon. It is here in form and emptiness, now, in *samsara*.

Theravada or Southern Buddhism

For many, the idea of Buddhism is most vividly represented by the orange-robed monk. Today, this robe – an ancient symbol of renunciation – is still worn by monks in Sri Lanka and southeast Asia: the countries where Theravada (Doctrine of the Elders) is the dominant school. While Mahayana (Great Vehicle) was adopted by the peoples to the north of India, most nations of south and southeast Asia inherited Theravada. Theravada derives from a conservative school of early Indian Hinayana (Small Vehicle), and this tradition, as codified in ancient Sri Lanka, is still practised in Burma, Sri Lanka, Laos, Thailand and Cambodia.

The secret of Theravada's longevity perhaps lies in three different tendencies: its strict adhererence to the letter of the Pali scriptures (see p.71); its flair for the creation of powerful monastic institutions and for sustaining ties with secular government; and its skill in co-existing with and absorbing elements of non-Buddhist folk religion. Contrastingly, since the 19th century, many Europeans have been drawn to rational and psychological elements in Theravada; it is partially these non-metaphysical aspects of the *dharma* (teaching) that have, in the past two decades, brought so many Westerners to Theravada meditation.

A view of Borobudur, the vast 9th-century monument in central Java. Massively ornamented with Buddhist scenes in full and half-relief, this mandala*-shaped temple-mountain is unique in Buddhist architectural history.*

Buddhism is established in Sri Lanka

The 3rd-century BC *Thuparama Dagaba at Anuradhapura, the oldest Sri Lankan* stupa: *said to enshrine the Buddha's collarbone and an eating bowl relic.*

Buddhism came to Sri Lanka in about 250BC, toward the end of Ashoka's rule in India. The missionary emperor had taken Buddhism to the far northwest and south of the subcontinent. According to the *Mahavamsa*, the colourful early history of Sri Lanka, it was one of Ashoka's sons, the monk Mahinda, who carried the *dharma* to the island. Before Mahinda's arrival there were several religions in Sri Lanka: mainly Brahmanism, ancestor worship and animistic nature cults.

As told in the *Mahavamsa*, Mahinda's mission began near Anuradhapura, the Sri Lankan capital. Encountering Mahinda and his seven companions, King Devanampiya-Tissa stopped to hear an account of the *dharma*. Convinced by Mahinda's discourse together with a dismal account of rebirth in *samsara*, the king invited him back to Anuradhapura, where the young monk preached in a park outside the city. Within days, the king had presented another park to the *sangha* (community): it was here that the Mahavihara, the Great Monastery, was founded.

"Is Buddhism now established here?" the king asked. Two texts describe the *bhikkhu*'s reply. In one, Mahinda says

The Kantaka cetiya, *an ancient Sri Lankan* stupa *(1st–2nd century* BC*), built at Mihintale on the site where Mahinda first preached. The rocky terrain (bottom right) provided caves for monks.*

the *dharma* would be established when there was a boundary (*sima*) round a monastery for "acts of the *sangha*".

"Great king," says Mahinda in the second account, "the *Sasana* [teaching] is established: but its roots are shallow."

"When will the roots deepen?"

"When a son born in Sri Lanka, of Sri Lankan parents, becomes a monk in Sri Lanka, studies the *Vinaya* in Sri Lanka and recites it in Sri Lanka, then the roots of the *Sasana* will go deep."

While the first story reflects orthodox monastic ceremonial, the second points to the close relationship that has long existed between Buddhism and Singhalese nationhood. For more than 2,000 years, most Singhalese people have identified Buddhism with being Sri Lankan. Also vital to this story is the image of the tree, so important to the symbology of early Buddhism. According to the *Mahavamsa*, the king, following his conversion, sent to India for a branch of the enlightenment tree at Bodh Gaya. A sister of Mahinda, the nun Sanghamitta, travelled south with a branch of the *bodhi* tree, and this was planted at Anuradhapura. The "roots" of the *dharma* thus soon gripped the island.

The bodhi *tree – a probable descendant of Sanghamitta's cutting – at Anuradhapura today.*

Temple of the Tooth, Kandy, 16th century. Daily rituals venerate the Buddha's tooth relic.

RELICS AND MONUMENTS FROM THE ANCIENT BUDDHIST KINGDOM

According to the Sri Lankan chronicles, Mahinda supervised construction of monastic buildings near Anuradhapura. Simultaneously, he sent to India for Buddhist relics. These, say the histories, included the Buddha's alms bowl and his right collarbone. Later a hair relic and, in the 4th century AD, the Buddha's tooth would be taken to Sri Lanka. The tooth is still preserved in the city of Kandy. To house the relics, *stupas* were built. For the collarbone, the Thuparama Dagaba was constructed at Anuradhapura in north-central Sri Lanka: the first *stupa* in the country. Much restored, the great dome, circled with old columns, is still to be seen at Anuradhapura, now a great park. During major festivals it is crowded with hundreds of thousands of devotees in family groups, who picnic happily among the ruins and offer *puja* at the *bodhi* tree.

With its *stupas*, monastic buildings, reservoirs and Buddha images, Anuradhapura is one of the world's great sacred sites. There are other important monuments nearby at Mihintale, the site of Mahinda's first sermon to King Devanampiya-Tissa. The ruins of the later capital at Polonnaruwa (9th century AD onwards), showing Hindu and Mahayana cultic influence, are yet more elaborate.

Theravada Buddhism in Sri Lanka

A temple precinct in modern Laos, where Theravada was introduced from Sri Lanka.

Sri Lanka is a mere ferry boat ride from the tip of south India: but in making that short crossing in the 3rd century BC, 2,000 years of southern Buddhist history became securely anchored. Buddhism would vanish from the Indian mainland by the 15th century. But in nearby Sri Lanka – as well as in Thailand, Burma, Laos and Cambodia – the Hinayana school of Buddhism called Theravada still flourishes.

Theravada (Doctrine of the Elders) was one of the earliest and most conservative Indian schools; by the mid-4th century BC, it had already split from the majority Mahasanghika community. The dispute centred on the nature of *arhats* (fully enlightened people). Could an *arhat* have erotic fantasies? Was it possible for someone who had had a nocturnal emission (wet dream) to go into *nirvana*? While the Mahasanghikas claimed monks with some imperfections might be *arhats*, the elders insisted an *arhat* was one in whom all blemishes were destroyed.

In the following centuries there were more divisions; and once Theravada was established in Sri Lanka, there were further schisms. The Mahavihara (Great Monastery) had two rival monasteries – with all but identical doctrines to its own – near Anuradhapura. And while Mahayana Buddhism, Hinduism and Tantra had their lesser places within the religious community, it was the elders of the Great Monastery who had decisive influence both in Sri Lanka and in southeast Asia.

However, pressure from outside forced change on the Sri Lankan *sangha* (monastic community). The first

The huge rock-cut Buddha at Avukana (9th century), with his right hand raised in the abhaya *("fear not" gesture).*

significant threat came in *c*.43BC when Sri Lanka was attacked by Tamil forces from the Indian mainland and for several years the island was ravaged by war and famine. It was during this period, according to the Sri Lankan chronicles, that monastic leaders determined to make Theravada texts secure. Even if the *sangha* were destroyed, at least the Buddha's word would survive the calamity. This was the moment when the Pali scriptures, until then largely preserved in the memories of *bhikkhus* (monks), were first written down.

One of the many ancient stupas *at Odong, north of Phnom Penh, capital of Cambodia from the 17th to 19th centuries.*

THE PALI SCRIPTURES

While vast quantities of Mahayana Sanskrit literature have been preserved in Tibetan and Chinese translations, most Hinayana texts in their original Indian languages have been lost. It is assumed that most of the Hinayana schools had their own canon of works, but only the Theravada canon, transcribed in the Pali language, has survived in its entirety. No one knows the origin of Pali or how exactly it originally related to Sanskrit or the language of Magadha which the Buddha may have spoken. But for two millennia Pali has served as the language of the Theravada scriptures and scriptural commentary, and as the learned language of southern Buddhists. The Theravada canon, the *Ti-pitaka* (Three Baskets; Sanskrit, *Tri-pitaka*), is as follows:

1. The *Vinaya* (Discipline), which consists of monastic rules (*Patimokha*), with commentaries and accounts of historical and legendary incidents giving rise to each rule.

2. The *Suttas* (Sanskrit, *Sutras*) in five groups (*nikaya*):

Digha-Nikaya (thirty-four long *suttas*);
Majjhima-Nikaya (152 middle-length *suttas*);
Samyutta-Nikaya (five books of linked *suttas* and verses);
Anguttara-Nikaya (eleven groups, each containing about ten *suttas*);
Khuddaka-Nikaya (about fifteen books, including the *Jataka* stories, the devotional poetry of the *Sutta-nipata*, *Udana* and *Elders' Verses*, and the much-translated *Dhammapada*.

3. The *Abdhidhamma* (Further *Dhamma*; Sanskrit, *Dharma*): seven books which systematize and categorize the elements of teaching in the two other "baskets". Pali literature is vastly increased by commentaries, most written by medieval Singhalese and Indian monastic scholars.

The Pali scriptures are mostly preserved on palm-leaf manuscripts. But this inscribed gold plate contains the earliest text found in Burma: vital evidence of Burmese Buddhism in the 5th century.

The spread of Theravada

The vast Buddha at the 12th-century Gal Vihara temple at Polonnaruwa. A Theravada monk arrives to conduct puja.

Of all Hinayana schools, Theravada has been the most historically successful. But since most early monasteries relied on strong royal support, Hinayana lost ground in India after the death of Ashoka; the rise of Mahayana in the 1st and 2nd centuries AD also contributed to its isolation. Even in its Sri Lankan stronghold, Theravada was marginalized for some centuries. A Buddhist revival in the 12th century under King Parakkramabahu (1153–86) re-established Theravada dominance until successive European invasions.

Theravada tradition had been preserved at the Mahavihara and two rival monasteries near Anuradhapura. A new monastic centre at Polonnaruwa in the 12th century launched a period of Theravada renewal in scholarship, political influence, art and architecture. In the same century, Theravada spread from Sri Lanka and was established in southeast Asia, initially in Burma, where Singhalese monks converted the king. Thailand followed a century later by similar royal diktat, while Cambodia and Laos adopted Theravada in the 14th century.

Thus as Buddhism died in its Indian homeland, Theravada took root in southeast Asia, where for the most part it has been dominant to this day.

Young Theravada monks with their eating bowls enter a temple gateway in Thailand.

Local women arrive with food offerings at the monastery. Monks must eat before noon.

Rangoon's Shwe Dagon pagoda (14th–15th century) is one of the most splendidly rich and intensively decorated buildings in southeast Asia. With its gilded spires and luxuriantly adorned shrines, it gleams on the city skyline as a "remembrance" (cetiya) *of the golden-faced Buddha. The spires, unique to Burma, are versions of the royal tiered umbrellas that surmounted early Indian* stupas.

THE GREAT WRITER AND TRANSLATOR BUDDHAGHOSA

Born in north India to a non-Buddhist family, Buddhaghosa was probably the single most influential thinker in the history of Theravada. Legends about Buddhaghosa come to us from chronicles such as the *Mahavamsa*, while the man himself is represented by a vast series of commentaries and translations which were composed at Anuradhapura.

The name Buddhaghosa means "voice of the Buddha", and tradition makes frequent play on this: "The Buddha established the religion, but it has found voice in Buddhaghosa," says one source; another text proclaims, "He was like the Buddha on earth." It is said that when the young *bhikkhu* arrived at Anuradhapura, he was subjected to a test before being given the freedom to read Singhalese commentaries to the scriptures. Asked to comment on a certain verse, Buddhaghosa sat down and wrote the *Visuddhi-magga* (Path of Purity), a lengthy volume on Buddhist meditation. This Pali classic was followed by his Pali translations of the *Tri-pitaka* commentaries (see p.71) from their original Singhalese and then by commentaries of his own. There has been little in Theravada thought or scriptural interpretation since the 5th century AD that does not carry the stamp of Buddhaghosa's authority.

THE HISTORICAL BASE OF THERAVADA BUDDHISM

"Abandoning violence to all living things ... one should wander alone as a rhinoceros horn," opens a famous poem in the *Sutta-nipata* (see p.71). The ideal of the world-renouncing *bhikkhu* (monk) figures large in some of the Theravada scriptures, but early Buddhist monasteries could never have survived without royal patronage and close ties with their neighbouring communities.

Buddhist recluses have always existed. But since the laity provide monks with food, clothes and medicine, even the most isolated *bhikkhus* tend to live within range of a village. The relationship between monks and laity is of mutual benefit. In return for alms, monks provide education and officiate at community festivals. This social relationship with the laity has always been of prime importance to Theravada.

In Thailand the influence of the monarchy has long been central; the royal family has been closely associated with Buddhism since the 19th century. The Thai people were fortunate to escape colonization by expanding Western powers. But in Sri Lanka the Theravada tradition was profoundly eroded by successive imperial rulers: the Portuguese in the 16th century, then the Dutch, and finally the British. A Buddhist revival in the late 19th century brought Sri Lankan Buddhism back to the centre of Singhalese consciousness.

Monks and laity in Theravada Buddhism

The ordination of monks in the Theravada *sangha* (monastic community) is believed to derive from an unbroken line dating from the Buddha himself. The *sangha* was traditionally described as having "four assemblies": monks, nuns, and male and female lay devotees (*upasakas*). The Theravada tradition of women's ordination was broken in the 5th century AD, and although women today can take the robe and live a monastic existence, they may not participate fully in the affairs of the *sangha*.

A nun at devotions at the Shwe Dagon pagoda in Rangoon, Burma.

The structure of monastic life is determined by rules set down in the "basket" of Theravada texts called the *Vinaya* (see p.71). Several versions evolved over the centuries but the only complete Hinayana version to survive is that in Pali. This was the code adopted by the Great Monastery at Anuradhapura, and Theravada monks in Sri Lanka and southeast Asia follow its rule to this day.

Ordination takes place in two stages. First, at the minimum age of eight, is a "going forth" from lay existence to the status of novice; this, after a period of training, may be followed by full ordination, at the minimum age of twenty. Novices follow the ten precepts (see p.41); the saffron-robed *bhikkhu* must obey the *Vinaya*'s 227 rules as set out in the *Patimokha*. Ordination is a simple process, and as a return to lay existence involves no dishonour, many men become monks for short periods. In Thailand, most boys have their heads shaved and are ordained at least once for a number of weeks; and many men return to robes for limited periods, especially during the three months of *vassa* (rainy season) when monastic life is at its most crowded and intense. Since all monastic life is governed by the *Vinaya*, the most important communal period is the day of observance (*uposatha*) when the

Thai monks at an ordination ceremony. They exchange the white robes of the lay devotee for the monastic yellow.

The ordination of monks is celebrated with brightly coloured banners, parasols and festively dressed elephants, as shown in this rural procession in Thailand.

Patimokha is recited. This happens twice a month at the new moon and full moon; on one of these days monks are enjoined to public confession of faults.

A *bhikkhu*'s routine is not confined to the boundaries (*sima*) within which monastic life is conducted. Even today, with many monasteries endowed with the necessities of life, monks walk out on their morning alms round, returning to eat before noon as the *Vinaya* demands. Others, especially in Thailand, travel between monasteries and spend time on pilgrimages to Buddhist shrines. Perhaps the greatest proportion of a monk's time is devoted to the laity – at funerals and other events requiring a monastic blessing, and providing both religious and secular education. In supporting *bhikkhus* with food and the "eight requisites" (including robes, razor, bowl, staff and water-strainer) lay people accumulate merit (*punna*); and in providing the laity with this opportunity, *bhikkhus* likewise accrue the *punna* that leads to a favourable rebirth.

THE "GREAT" AND "LITTLE" TRADITIONS

Rather than try invalidating the pre-Buddhist religions of Sri Lanka and southeast Asia, the "great" tradition of monastic Buddhism has always accommodated itself to folk belief. Thus most monks, however learned, participate in a popular "village *dharma*", which may be a mixture of Buddhism, spirit cults and ancestor worship, with borrowings from Mahayana, Tantra and Hinduism. In Burma, the old religion of the thirty-six spirits (*nats*) has been incorporated into popular Buddhism, the Buddha being acknowledged "the thirty-seventh *nat*". Learned monks see no reason to devalue popular cults and routinely officiate at offerings (*puja*) to images of mixed religious origin. Some monks also specialize in non-orthodox occult practices such as astrology, exorcism and divination. This open frontier between the "great" and "little" traditions has lent Theravada a great vigour, tolerance and flexibility through the centuries.

Buddhist monuments of southeast Asia

Preceded by Hinduism and the Mahayana, Theravada came to Burma and southeast Asia by the mid-5th century AD, but took some centuries to become established. The endurance of religious groups depended on the patronage of royalty, and, like Indian monarchs, southeast Asian kings practised religious tolerance. Theravada became securely based in Burma once monasteries and *cetiyas* ("reminders of the Buddha" in *stupa* form) were under royal protection. By the 8th century, there was a Burmese capital on the northerly Pagan flatlands; but Burma was still divided. Unification came in the 11th century when King Anawrahta (1044–77) invaded the south and brought Theravada monks, the southern Mon royalty and Mon artisans to Pagan. Two centuries of stupendous building then followed, synthesizing Burmese and Mon styles with Indian architectural models. Pagan enjoyed unparalleled splendour during this period; and although the city was conquered by Kublai Khan in 1287, and its teak-built palaces and monasteries have gone, the hot dry climate has preserved the remains of 5,000 religious buildings.

The splendour of Pagan today lies in its extraordinary scale, the beautiful forms of half-ruined brick *cetiyas* and the blaze of white stucco on the great restored Ananda temple (*c.*AD1105). Pagan's architectural styles were varied. But a three-part *cetiya* pattern came to dominate: a stepped pyramidal base surmounted by a drum- or bell-shaped *stupa* and topped with a spire. Viewed as a whole, the Pagan *cetiya* simultaneously suggested Mount Meru (the cosmic axis) and the sacred mountain homes – in particular Mount Popa – of

Two great temples of Pagan: left, the graceful 11th-century Ananda temple with its Indian-style tower and surrounding stupas*; right, That-byin-nyu temple (the "Omniscient").*

An aerial view of Borobudur, the spectacular 9th-century Buddhist monument in central Java.

CENTRAL JAVA: CHANDI MENDUT AND BOROBUDUR

While Theravada dominated southeast Asia, Mahayana and Vajrayana took root in Indonesia. Central Java's Buddhist monuments are among the world's architectural masterpieces. Two of these (both *c.*AD800) are particularly spectacular. One is Chandi Mendut: a splendidly decorated stone pyramid with an inner shrine containing huge images of a seated Buddha and two *bodhisattavas*.

But perhaps the most overwhelming of any Buddhist "mountain" is Borobudur. The structure consists of five diminishing square terraces. From the topmost square, three round terraces ringed with open-work *stupas* containing life-sized Buddhas ascend. The monument's summit is a round, empty *stupa*. An aerial view shows that Borobudur was intended to be a *mandala* (see pp.144–5), and like a *mandala* the building was presumably a meditation object. Borobudur's design is in three parts. The lowest represents *kamadhatu*: the sense-world of *samsara*. The second stage represents *rupadhatu*, the world of deities. Finally there is *arupadhatu*, the formlesss sphere of enlightenment. Each of the square terraces is an ambulatory reached by a staircase thickly decorated with reliefs illustrating Buddhist texts, and symbols appropriate to each level. As devotees walk round and upward they rise through a cosmos embracing both Buddhist history and a model of spiritual progress. Walkers may perhaps not achieve the *nirvana* of the highest stratum; but they will have experienced the range of human possibility. Since Vajrayana teaches that the lowest and highest levels of consciousness are the same (see pp.138–9), this physical contact with the *mandala* of Borobudur provides an intimate experience of Buddhist wholeness.

The upper terrace at Borobudur with a large Buddha and open-work stupas *in the background.*

indigenous Burmese *nat* deities. To build a *cetiya* was an act of great merit, for the sacred "mountain" that it represented would be a home for Buddhist and *nat* divinities.

Many *cetiyas*, like their Indian Buddhist prototypes, were originally solid. Some were later hollowed out, in the style of the Hindu temple, for shrines and passages. The surfaces of *stupas* were splendidly decorated: the white stucco abounding in garlands, urns, lotuses, sea-monsters and other iconography derived from Indian Buddhist stone-carving. Lavish gilding – most strikingly in the flame finials so characteristic of Burmese roof architecture – suggested dragon-like upward aspiration and the burning endeavour (*tejas*) of monastic asceticism.

Buddhism in China

The history of Chinese Buddhism provides a fascinating tableau of both continuity and transformation. As Buddhism travelled east, the Indian *dharma* maintained a great degree of integrity; but with the advance into Chinese territory, a contest developed. China had, in Confucianism and Taoism, long-established traditions: to survive, Buddhism must become Chinese. The flexibility of the *dharma* was thus tested as never before. What helped eventually to fix Buddhism in Chinese culture were the great translations of Sanskrit texts, which gave rise to a proliferation of new ideas culminating in China's most original contribution to Buddhism: Ch'an, or early Zen. Ch'an, the school of direct meditational experience, arose partly in reaction to academic learning. Both currents, intuitive and scholastic, had far-reaching influence on the development of Buddhism.

Pressure on the *dharma* also came from indigenous ideas. Buddhism never died in China, but the past 500 years have seen the mutual absorption of major schools. A syncretic religion became widespread, drawing from Buddhist schools and from Taoist and Confucian traditions. In the 20th century these trends have been devastated by ideas from the West and by Chinese communism. Buddhism nevertheless still flourishes in Taiwan, Hong Kong and Singapore, and is making a recovery in mainland China.

A 13th-century silk scroll from the Yuan dynasty depicting the Buddha, surrounded by his mourning followers, in parinirvana. *The monk under the jewelled tree at the top left strikes a gong bowl three times, signifying Buddha,* dharma *and* sangha.

The eastward spread of Buddhism

Ancient Buddhism was often an evangelizing religion. But it took 300 years from the death of the Buddha for the *dharma* to move beyond India. The Indian emperor Ashoka was converted to Buddhism in *c.*260BC (see pp.58–9) and some twenty years later he sent monks on a successful mission to Sri Lanka. The missionaries that he sent to the kingdom of Gandhara (north Pakistan, east Afghanistan), which Alexander the Great had conquered in 327BC, were equally successful. The Persian armies that Alexander threw out and the Greek colonists he left behind had imported their own Zoroastrian and Greek ideas. These influences, mixed with cults surrounding local gods, quickly absorbed Buddhism and helped transform it. It was from here, via the cosmopolitan interchange between India and its northwestern neighbours, that many ideas of both Hinayana and Mahayana were channelled east toward China.

Trade between two great powers, the Roman and Chinese, was largely responsible for the eastward expansion of Buddhism. The caravan routes skirting the central Asian desert were served by a series of prosperous oasis towns which the Chinese finally brought under their protection from attack by Huns and Turks *c.*50BC. Here, Buddhist monks and pilgrims settled, built monasteries and proselytized among Turkish, Mongolian, Nestorian Christian and Chinese residents and travellers. From these townships in the desert, Buddhism spread naturally into the western provinces of China.

The existence of these central Asian Buddhist centres was brought fully to light only early this century by European scholars, in particular Sir Aurel Stein, who led three long expeditions through the Taklamakan desert. Important Mahayana Buddhist manuscripts in Sanskrit and central Asian languages such as Khotanese were excavated from shrines and monasteries that had been buried in the sand for almost two millennia. A completely new area of Buddhist culture, linking India and Gandhara in the west and Chinese Buddhism to the east, was uncovered.

This 10th-century votive silk hanging from Dunhuang shows the bodhisattva *Avalokiteshvara on a lotus, a spray of willow in his raised hand and the figure of Amitabha Buddha in his headdress. The donor of the hanging and his sister are depicted on either side. The inscription prays for peace, and for rebirth in the Pure Land.*

THE DUN-HUANG CAVE SHRINES

Stein's most spectacular discoveries were at the oasis town of Dun-huang on the edge of Chinese Turkestan. This was China's most westerly outpost, and it marked the beginning of the Silk Road through central Asia. A significant Buddhist monastic centre from the 4th century AD until the Tibetan invasion in 759, Dun-huang consists of hundreds of caves hollowed out of a cliff and filled with magnificent wall paintings and clay sculptures. The frescoes in the earlier caves are strongly influenced by central Asian, Gandharan and even European styles. In later caves, a recognizably Chinese idiom has evolved. One of the caves – carefully sealed by devotees over 1,000 years ago – contained, among other treasures, perfectly preserved ritual banners and manuscripts which attest the importance of Dun-huang as a centre of Buddhist scholarship and ceremonial.

An 8th-century AD painting from Dun-huang, showing the Buddha preaching on the Vulture Peak, where he delivered the Lotus Sutra.

Third-century Buddhist iconography in Greco-Roman style from Gandhara (Swat Valley, Pakistan) showing the Buddha's parinirvana.

THE IMAGE OF THE BUDDHA

The thriving cultures of Gandhara, fed by the gold and silver trade from India and silk from China, produced a unique Buddhist art and iconography. The Greek stone-carvers and metal-workers of Gandhara – heirs to the conquering Alexander – were probably the first to depict the Buddha as a human being. Before, Indian craftsmen had depicted him symbol-ically. An empty throne or a royal umbrella represented the Buddha's non-temporal kingship. A lotus inscribed on a footprint symbolized his transcendence and purity. Now, in the 1st century AD, the Buddha appeared in the form of a man. Strangely, however, Greco-Roman stylistic formulae almost completely dominated. These were semi-Europeanized Buddhas, often with wavy hair and curling moustaches. Earlier Gandharan figures wear Hellenistic drapery; later figures are Roman in appearance, probably made by craftsmen from Rome's Middle Eastern empire.

Bodhisattva *with halo, robed and coiffed by carvers of Gandhara, 3rd century AD.*

Confucianism

Confucius is here represented with patrician serenity by an artist of the 7th century AD.

Of the three great ways of thought in ancient China – Confucian, Taoist and Buddhist – the first two were native to China, while Buddhism, alien "wisdom from the west", often had to struggle for admission to Chinese society. Certainly, in its central 1,000 years of development in China, Buddhism altered the course of history and evolved some uniquely Chinese forms. But Buddhism also suffered periods of repression, and the imported religion was eventually marginalized by the native traditions.

The foundation of Chinese philosophy lay in the teachings of Confucius (K'ung Fu-tzu). Born in 551BC into a period of disorder among the feudal states of the Chou dynasty, Confucius based his teaching on the cultivation of morality, order, learning and tradition. Just as the Buddha, teaching during the same period, defined the word *brahmin* (person of priestly caste) purely in terms of virtue (see pp.34–5), so Confucius taught that a man was a "gentleman" (*chun-tzu*) only if he embraced *jen* (humanity, virtue). If all people followed this path of mildness and benevolence, the moral order of the state could be reclaimed.

The teaching of Confucius reinforced a Chinese preoccupation with the idealized past of righteous kings who had founded the Chou dynasty. During this period the five Chinese ("Confucian") classics were believed to have come into existence. These were the *Book of Changes* (*I Ching*), the *Book of History*, the *Book of Odes*, the *Book of Rites*, and the *Spring and Autumn Annals*. Confucius taught that the study of these texts – which ranged from the oracular to folk poetry, history and descriptions of ethical and ritual good conduct – was indispensable to the man of *jen*. The highest calling for such men involved both studying the classics and following a political career. Such pursuits would lead to the re-establishment of the orderly world that the classics described or represented. In this way, the entire state, from emperor to peasant, would be brought into harmony and the resulting moral-political harmony would, in turn, harmonize with the moral order of heaven (*t'ien*).

Complementing this preoccupation with ancient lore, Confucius taught an ethic which placed the family at the centre of secular and ceremonial life. And

Confucius and Lao Tzu sit in imagined conversation, Confucius at the centre of a civilized terrace, Lao Tzu framed in a tranquil landscape.

HAN CONFUCIANISM

By the 2nd century BC, Confucianism had become the Chinese state system. The oral teachings of Confucius were preserved in the *Analects*, and these, along with the five classics, served as a basis of Han dynasty statecraft. According to Han theory, the emperor, "Son of Heaven", ruled by heaven's mandate. As long as he ruled according to heaven's will, there was peace and prosperity. The empire was administered by a bureaucracy of officials trained in the Confucian classics. These functionaries supervised state rituals and maintained "harmony" by ensuring that everyone in society performed, as Confucius taught, according to their function.

But the humane and flexible teachings of Confucius were rigidified under Han to its own detriment. Rational Confucian indifference to the supernatural lost ground to superstition. Most importantly, the value of the individual became submerged in a system which viewed the masses simply as a reflex of the emperor, his bureaucracy and the imperial order. Dissatisfied with such abstractions, people turned to other religions: first to the Tao, and later to Buddhism.

central to the family were the souls of its own ancestors. These family souls lived in heaven with the deity Shang-ti (Lord on High), and their spiritual protection was sought through sacrifices that were described in the *Book of Rites*. But Confucius was himself concerned less with ritual and spirits than with humanistic ethics; and these, along with the five classics, informed the major part of Chinese thought for the next two millennia.

The stone stele and burial mound at the tomb of Confucius which was erected in 1443, in Qufu, Shandong province.

Taoism

Taoism is the second of the great native Chinese philosophies. *Tao*, like the word *dharma* in Buddhist Sanskrit, means several things. To the Confucian it denotes "the proper way of action and morality". In philosophical Taoism it has three linked meanings: the natural world; spontaneous freedom from social convention; and, most important, absolute reality – the essence and the source of life infusing all phenomena.

Philosophical Taoism was non-institutional. The Taoist sage, whose practice lay in "naturalness" (*tzu-jan*) and contemplation, had no use for rites and temples. Thus while the "gentleman" Confucian cultivated learning, family and state harmony, the Taoist sought solitude in nature and repudiated convention and religious texts. The subtle, all-pervading *tao* could be apprehended only through first-hand experience.

The inspiration for philosophical Taoism came from two works of literature. The first, by the legendary Lao Tzu, was the *Tao-te Ching*: a beautiful, enigmatic book, which, through paradox and veiled allusion, traces the workings of the *tao*, and evokes the quietist joy of a life dedicated to its immanence in all things. The other great text was a collection of essays, poems and stories by Chuang Tzu, who wrote in the 3rd century BC. Whereas parts of the *Tao-te Ching* suggest that the perfect ruler should govern – in benign *laissez-faire* – by the *tao*, Chuang Tzu rejects politics and urges a return to artless, primordial social simplicity.

The lofty but playful idiom of philosophical Taoism appealed largely to the intelligentsia who, in the face of 3rd-century imperial decay and the ossification of Han Confucianism (see p.83), sought new spiritual solutions. Around AD250, the Han dynasty slipped into chaos and a Taoist revival took place.

This brought the ideas of the two classics, and the sometimes startling behaviour of Taoist sages, directly into polite circles. One Taoist used to sit at home naked and get drunk. "Heaven and earth are my dwelling," he said to visitors who complained, "and my house is my trousers. Why are you all coming into my trousers?" Such was the subversive wit of neo-Taoists, hovering between love of society and withdrawal from its conventions.

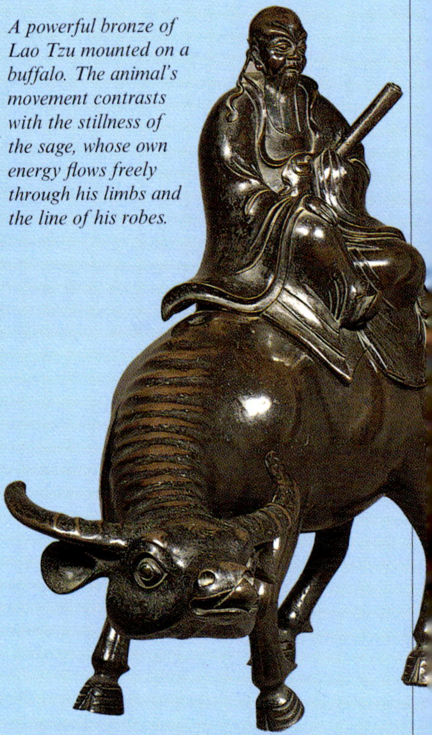

A powerful bronze of Lao Tzu mounted on a buffalo. The animal's movement contrasts with the stillness of the sage, whose own energy flows freely through his limbs and the line of his robes.

TAOISTS AT THE END OF THE HAN DYNASTY

In AD311, the Chinese capital Chang'an fell to the Huns. The emperor fled south, and for the next 300 years China was traumatically divided between the north, which was controlled by the "barbarians", and the south, which came under a series of unstable Chinese administrations.

Much of the intelligentsia escaped south with the court, and the spectacular mountain landscape of southern China became a new source of contemplative inspiration for Taoists. But for many of the exiled, demoralized elite, mystical Taoism degenerated into fashionable salon talk. It was, none the less, among these neo-Taoists that Buddhist ideas, now finding their way into southern China, found acceptance. *Shunyata* (emptiness; see pp.62–3) of Buddhist Mahayana was seen to coincide with the Taoist *wu*, that "silent non-being which is the source and basis of all things".

A painting of the emperor Liu Pang (256–195BC), who established the Han dynasty.

MAGICAL TAOISM

A popular movement also calling itself Taoist evolved alongside philosophical Taoism in the 3rd century BC. Resorting to special diets, the ingestion of alchemical potions such as cinnabar (a mercuric sulphide) and breathing exercises, occultists allied vaguely to Taoist theory sought to contact "deities" in their own bodies and thus transcend death. As Buddhism penetrated China and absorbed elements of philosophical Taoism, so popular Taoism, in an attempt to hold its ground, adopted Buddhist rituals and even texts. But since it increasingly took on magical beliefs, it lost credit with many of those who, in a troubled period, had clutched at its promises.

An 18th-century Chinese watercolour of a Taoist "master of the heavens", his robe embroidered with magical symbols. He holds a cup of immortal elixir. The streaming lines express fiercely dedicated spiritual freedom.

The beginnings of Chinese Buddhism

Han dynasty emperor Siuen Li with scholars translating texts. China, 17th century.

Buddhism started to penetrate China in c.AD50, and within the next hundred years Buddhist monks from India and central Asia had begun to establish their presence. At its height, the Chinese Han dynasty (206BC to AD220) had brought prosperity to an expanding empire. Chinese imperial self-confidence centred on the "Son of Heaven" – the prince at his court in Chang'an – who united the trinity of heaven, earth and humanity. But by the 1st century AD, the Han dynasty was seriously weakened. An increasingly powerful land-owning nobility eroded imperial control, imposing vast tax burdens on the peasant classes. Famine, plague and natural disasters swept through an empire already swarming with displaced people. Rebellions supported by Taoist leaders were followed by wars. The intervention of a new dynastic family, the Chin, did little to restore social and economic order. When the Huns invaded north China in AD311, the court fled south and the country was torn in half.

This social, economic and political crisis was a perfect seedbed for a new

Chinese imperial disfavour sometimes resulted in religious persecution. In this 17th-century painting, an emperor hurls scholars into a pit and bundles their books away. Buddhism was a target of such treatment from AD*842 to 845 in the otherwise strongly Buddhist T'ang dynasty.*

EARLY CHINESE INTEREST IN BUDDHISM

Just as Buddhism had found its way to China via the Silk Road from the west, so it spread along the internal trade routes within China itself. The first Chinese emperors to encounter Buddhist monks gave them tentative, limited patronage in case the Buddha was a powerful deity. Problems of translation from Indian languages to Chinese meant that the *dharma* was most easily taught as a means of acquiring magical powers and salvation: this appealed especially to Taoists in search of immortality. And it was often Taoist words that were used in the translation of Buddhist terminology. For example, *tao* (the way, the truth) became the equivalent of *dharma* (the teaching) or *bodhi* (enlightenment); *wu-wei* (non-action) was used for *nirvana*. Confucian terms were also borrowed. The Buddhist Sanskrit *sila* (morality) was translated by *hsiao-hsun* (filial obedience). In this way, Buddhism gradually took on a Chinese flavour.

CHINESE OBJECTIONS TO BUDDHISM

The Chinese had several reasons to resist Buddhism. First and foremost, the new religion was imported, and therefore "barbarian"; and as Buddhism was not mentioned in the Confucian classics it was doubly non-Chinese. Confucians had a further difficulty: since Buddhist monks were celibate, they could not take part in family life which laid so much stress on filial piety. Buddhist asceticism was also foreign to a Chinese culture of aesthetic and sensual pleasures.

Whereas on the one hand Buddhism had no formulae for the immortality sought by Taoists, it was alien to Confucians in two major respects. First, the doctrine of rebirth was impossible to reconcile with the Confucian notion of a heaven from which the ancestors bestowed blessings on their descendants. Second, because Buddhist monks acknowledged no secular authority, they refused to show their respect to the Chinese emperor by bowing.

These social and cultural factors made the progress of Buddhism through educated Chinese society relatively slow. And, although the "wisdom from the west" eventually took hold and lasted for 1,000 years, many of these same difficulties would ultimately bring the influence of Buddhism to an end.

religion. And when the educated classes tried to interpret the ills that imperial Confucianism had previously kept at bay, many found an answer from the Buddhist monks who had started to preach in their city centres.

A small number of proselytizing Buddhist monks in a vast country with ancient native traditions faced an immense task. Buddhist missionaries within India and central Asia had spread their ideas in largely non-literate societies. In China they confronted a culture steeped in literary and philosophical traditions which formed the very foundations of society.

The period of domestication in China

*A legendary universal "emperor of righteousness" (*cakravartin*), meditating, flanked by attendants with parasol and flywhisk.*

During the 300 years of division betweeen north and south China, Chinese Buddhism developed in several distinct ways. Converts to Buddhism in the south were drawn both to Hinayana (Small Vehicle) and Mahayana (Great Vehicle). Hinayana stressed a spiritual method which, through study of Indian texts and methodically organized meditation practice, moved gradually toward the goal of enlightenment. Mahayana, by contrast, offered a method in which sudden enlightenment, a Buddhist vision of totality, became possible. Chinese converts whose previous affiliation had been largely scholastic and Confucian tended to be more at home with the Hinayana school. Those who had followed the more intuitive and non-ritualistic Taoist path had greater sympathy with the Mahayana. The monasteries, hermitages and temples of both schools which established themselves in southern China were subsidized by rich Buddhist families and, when possible, by the imperial court. Southern emperors were shrewdly offered the example of legendary Indian "emperors of righteousness" (*cakravartins*; see p.11), and in AD517 one particularly enthusiastic Buddhist monarch went so far as to abolish all the relatively new Taoist temples which were continuing to compete with those of the Buddhists.

In northern China, the establishment of Buddhism was dependent on the whim of alien rulers. Buddhist missionaries played on the credulity of these new non-Chinese monarchs. A certain monk from the Indian northwest "knew that the Hun chieftain would not understand profound doctrine but would be able to recognize magical power as evidence for the potency of Buddhism. Thereupon, he took his begging bowl, filled it with water, burned incense, and recited a *mantra* over it. In a moment there sprang up a blue lotus whose brightness and colour dazzled the eyes." By demonstrating such powers, the Buddhists gained the protection they needed to spread their doctrine in the north. The fact that Buddhism was still relatively foreign, without links to entrenched native Chinese interests, made it especially attractive to the non-Chinese rulers. With no organized Taoist opposition, and a Buddhist acceptance of ancestor cults to make

Buddhism less foreign to Confucians, Buddhism swept through China in the 4th and 5th centuries AD. The same period also saw vast endowments to Buddhist institutions. Monasteries and temples, often on an enormous scale, operated as centres of teaching, philosophy, commerce and charity. By the mid-5th century, Buddhist institutions had become so strong that Confucian traditionalists and Taoists re-entering from the south twice persuaded the emperor to restrict Buddhist power. None the less, Buddhism continued to grow and to develop its important native schools of thought, eventually reaching its great flowering in the T'ang dynasty of the 7th to 10th centuries AD (see pp.94–7).

This 9th-century painting from Dun-huang shows the scholar Hsuan-tsang, China's greatest pilgrim to India. After travelling for sixteen years, he returned in AD645 to translate the manuscripts he had acquired on his journey.

THE GREAT TRANSLATORS

Anxious to understand the sources of the Buddhist *dharma*, Chinese converts sought to acquire Indian Buddhist texts. The difficulty in obtaining these was matched, however, with the fact that most were in Sanskrit, a language that has no connection with Chinese. The complex, abstract Indian texts were also incompatible with the Chinese preference for concrete, direct thinking and many had already been partially translated using a misleading native Chinese terminology. Several outstanding translators helped to solve this problem. The greatest was Kumarajiva, who in AD401 established an institute of translation in the northern capital, Chang'an. Hundreds of copyists and editors as well as specialists in Sanskrit and philosophy were employed. This project enabled the production of Chinese versions of the Buddhist texts that were free of Taoist and Confucian interpretation. Thus the way opened for the development of Buddhist thought in the Chinese language.

From the Chinese translation of the Diamond Sutra, *the first book ever printed (9th century).*

The T'ien-t'ai and Flower Garland schools

The T'ien-t'ai school was named after "Heavenly Terrace" mountain in south China where Chih-i, its founder, lived and taught in the 6th century AD. The Flower Garland school (Hua-yen), which shared elements of T'ien-t'ai's Mahayana doctrine, evolved slightly later in north China.

Chinese Buddhists had, by the 6th century, received vast quantities of Indian texts. But the scholars who translated these works were all too aware of the difficulty of judging their relative authenticity. Chih-i responded to this confusion by systematizing the canon into a series of stages and periods in which the Buddha had gradually unveiled his doctrine. These stages began with "simple" Hinayana doctrines and culminated in the *Lotus Sutra* (see right), from which T'ien-t'ai derived some of its beliefs. The Flower Garland school based its ideas on the *Ghandavuya* (Flower Garland) from the *Avatamsaka Sutra* which the Buddha was believed to have delivered immediately after his enlightenment (see pp.24–5). Both T'ien-t'ai and the Flower Garland sects drew their support from the educated classes and both emphasized meditation and philosophical speculation. T'ien-t'ai also offered its adherents the personal salvation proclaimed by the *Lotus Sutra*.

The Buddha standing on a lotus flower pedestal. Behind him is a delicately engraved leaf-shaped mandorla.

These two Chinese schools re-interpreted the Mahayana *shunyata* position (the emptiness that represents the absolute; see pp.62–3). T'ien-t'ai taught that all phenomena are inseparable from the absolute (*shunyata*), and that "in every particle of dust, in every thought-moment, the whole universe is contained". The Flower Garland school asserted that all phenomena in the universe arose simultaneously. These phenomena are empty and yet contain both absolute (static, eternal) and relative (impermanent) aspects. When asked to explain this apparent dualism by the empress Wu Tse-t'ien (*c.*AD704), the sage Fa-tsang pointed to a palace statue and responded with his famous *Essay on the Golden Lion*. In this, the gold is a symbol of all-pervading *li* (the absolute, *shunyata*); the lion image is *shih*, a tangible phenomenon infused with *li*.

SCHOLARSHIP AND ADAPTATION

Given the ancient Chinese preference for synthesis and flexibility, the doctrines of "emptiness" and "mind only" (see pp.62–3) were, unadapted, too extreme to last long. The sects that arose in 5th-century China often represented groups with an interest in a particular text, such as the *Lotus* or the *Garland Sutra*. These were studied, copied, memorized and taught; this emphasis on learning expressed intellectual curiosity as well as religious affiliation. There was thus little conflict between schools and, like many 20th-century Westerners who sample the teachings of several gurus, many devotees in ancient China travelled the country to study different doctrines without allying themselves with one.

THE *LOTUS SUTRA*

The *Lotus of the Good Law* was one of the great Mahayana *sutras* to be translated into Chinese from Sanskrit in the 5th to 6th centuries AD. Possibly the most influential text in Buddhist history, the *Lotus Sutra* promises salvation for all beings.

At the heart of this long volume of poetry, sermons and allegories, glows the compassion of a Buddha whose central concern is earthly suffering. The Buddha's meditation is no longer directed at personal enlightenment. Instead, "by meditation and wisdom, the Buddha saves all beings". But everyone is able to reach Buddhahood – not just those who, through thought and meditation, have reached a comprehension of the *dharma* (doctrine). It is the suffering masses who may have "merely folded their hands" or "uttered *namo* [homage] to the Buddha". These people will "dwell in pure wisdom. None will fail to become the Buddha."

The *Lotus* has other celebrated attributes. One chapter contains a powerful allegory on *samsara* (the cycle of rebirth), with *samsara* metaphorically depicted as a house of horrors. Children are playing inside when it suddenly catches fire. The house-owner lures the children out and thus, by "skilful means", saves them. The house-owner is the compassionate Buddha who beguiles us "children" from our bewitching samsaric play to the safety of *nirvana*.

A page from a 9th–10th-century illustrated booklet version of the Lotus Sutra*, from the Dun-huang cave shrines.*

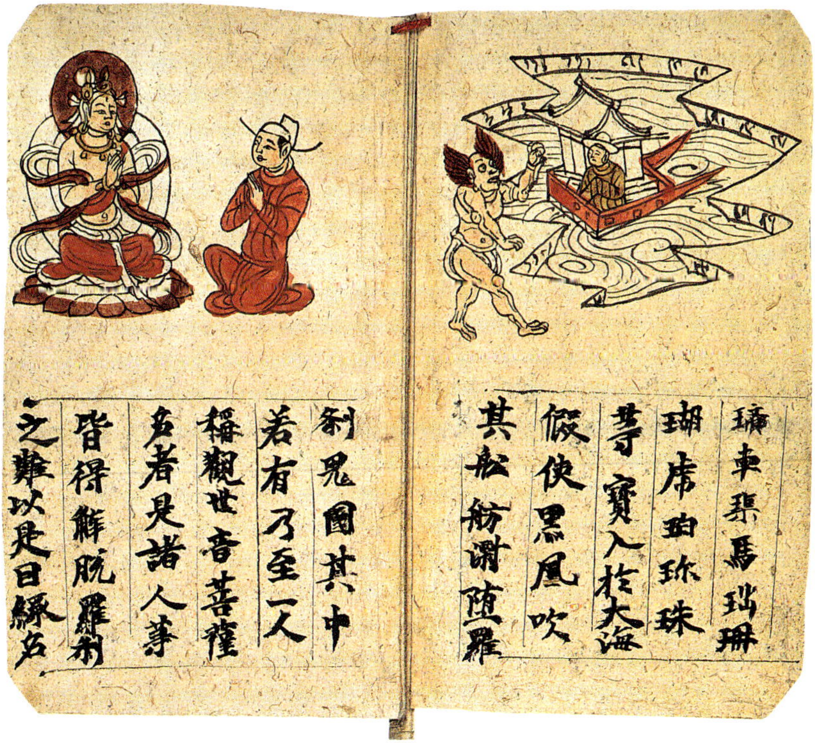

The Pure Land sect

A huge Amitabha Buddha in marble from the Sui dynasty of the 6th century. Originally the right hand would have gestured reassurance, the left hand liberality.

Pure Land is a devotional Buddhism offering an escape from the cycle of rebirth through faith in a deified Buddha. Mahayana speculation in the 1st and 2nd centuries AD had developed a cosmology that was far more extensive than anything that had been discussed in earlier Buddhism. The Buddha had taught that "the world, its origin and cessation is contained in our fathom-long carcass"; Mahayanists proposed the existence of infinite worlds, each containing Buddhas and *bodhisattvas.*

These "Buddha fields" are paradisal realms each presided over by a Buddha. The most celebrated of these heavens is the western paradise known as Sukhavati, "happy" or "pure" land. This is the dwelling of the Buddha Amitabha (Unlimited Radiance). Two Mahayana texts called the *Sukhavati-vyua* describe this heaven. It is a paradise where "there is neither physical nor mental pain ... it is filled with gods and men who will never be reborn except as *bodhisattvas.*" Among the pleasures in Sukhavati are musical and fragrant rivers; blossoms that fall in perfectly regulated showers; lakes of many-coloured lotuses; jewelled trees; splendid architecture, and other wish-fulfilling although non-erotic pleasures. Above all, in this paradise, everyone may hear the Buddha preaching.

An illustration from the 10th-century Ten Kings Sutra *showing the evil punished and the good rewarded by one of the kings and his attendants.*

This poetic account of Buddhist salvation is perhaps construed as an easily accessible version of *nirvana*. But whereas according to Hinayanists, *nirvana* might be realized only by those who have struggled to achieve it over many lives, Sukhavati can be entered, according to one text, by anyone, regardless of their *karma* (see pp.16–17). According to the other *Sukhavati-vyua* text, meritorious deeds are a condition of salvation. Otherwise, all that is required is to keep the name of Amitabha undisturbed in thought for up to seven nights; or, on the point of death, to think of Amitabha.

Many Mahayanists in the 3rd century believed that after the Buddha's death there was a decline, over three periods, in the vigour of *dharma* teaching. Partly on account of the political instability

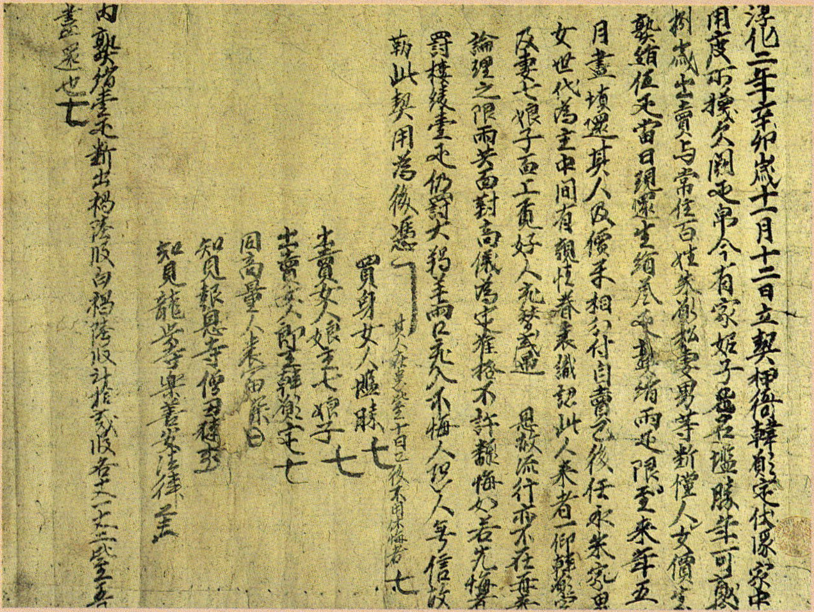

A page of manuscript from the Ten Kings Sutra, *from Dun-huang cave shrines, 10th century.*

which followed the collapse of the Han dynasty (AD220) and because of difficulties in mastering an ever-increasing complexity of doctrines, many Chinese Buddhists shared this belief and assumed that they lived in the period of Final Degenerate Law. A sure way to salvation might therefore be through faith in Amitabha rather than in the laborious progress toward enlightenment. Pure Land, with its emphasis on faith and the recital of the *mantra* "*Nan-mo A-mi-t'o*" (Homage to Amitabha Buddha) thus became the most widespread of all Chinese Buddhist disciplines. And Pure Land worship was never simply confined to the popular sphere. To this day, adherents of other, more rarefied, Chinese Buddhist sects, such as T'ien-t'ai, combine meditation practice with Pure Land devotion.

AVALOKITESHVARA BECOMES THE CHINESE KUAN-YIN

An emanation of the Amitabha Buddha and a co-resident of the western paradise was Avalokiteshvara, the *bodhisattva* of compassion. The Sanskrit name Avalokiteshvara means "the lord who looks down", a term suggestive of the *bodhisattva*'s loving care for humanity from his celestial height. Mahayana Buddhist enlightenment is often conceived as the wisdom of a Buddha combined with the compassion of a *bodhisattva.* In Tantric Buddhism (see p.139) this "unity in duality" was conceived in terms of "female wisdom" conjoined with "male compassion". Traditionally, Avalokiteshvara was male, and in Tibetan Buddhism he acquired a female consort called the White Tara. By the 10th century, Chinese Pure Land Buddhists had transformed Avalokiteshvara and the White Tara into Sung-tzu Kuan-yin: "Avalokiteshvara, giver of children". Kuan-yin, the figure "clad in white", remains the most popular figure in Chinese Pure Land devotionalism.

Ch'an: the school of meditation

The word *ch'an* is Chinese for the Sanskrit term *dhyana* (meditation); in Japan it developed as Zen, the form in which it is most widely known in the West today. Although other schools of Chinese Buddhism emphasize meditation, the practice of introspective sitting is, above all else, central to Ch'an. Unlike other Chinese schools, Ch'an abjures ritual, and even the authority of texts. In this sense, it is akin to Taoism: both paths teach a way to enlightenment that is "natural", spontaneous and independent of scholarly trappings.

Ch'an developed at a time of serene prosperity at the beginning of the great T'ang dynasty (AD618–907). This period, as the poetry of Li Po and Tu Fu attests, was a time of glorious achievement in the arts. The witty, profound teachings of the Ch'an masters were an integral part of this creative milieu. When other forms of Buddhism were suppressed in the late T'ang persecutions of AD845, Ch'an, with Pure Land Buddhism (see pp.92–3), managed to survive. Pure Land survived due to its popular appeal. Ch'an endured because it owned little that could be destroyed and because most Ch'an monks worked as part of their religious practice and could not be condemned as monastic parasites.

The Ch'an school was presided over by a succession of patriarchs, the first of whom was probably an Indian monk called Bodhidharma who is said to have arrived in southern China *c.*AD520.

A 13th-century ink drawing of the Taoist poet Li Po reciting. His famous line, "drunkenly I chase the brook-moon", beautifully expresses the self-mockery of Taoist and Ch'an sages all too conscious of their delusion.

Rebuffed by the southern court, Bodhidharma retreated north, where he sat open-eyed in front of a wall for nine years, before agreeing to teach. Bodhidharma's insistence on silent meditation was such that he refused to take pupils, until a monk called Hui'ke cut off his own arm to prove his earnestness. It was probably Bodhidharma who brought the Mahayanist *Lankavatara Sutra* to Chinese Buddhism.

Of special importance to Ch'an is the *Lankavatara*'s doctrine of non-duality. "All things," says the *Lankavatara*, in a synthesis of "emptiness" and "mind only" doctrines (see pp.62–3), "are not-two". The "Buddha-mind" that meditators seek within themselves is identical with the unitary, absolute, primordial emptiness. Another element that Ch'an took up from the *Lankavatara* is that the *dharma* may be non-verbally transmitted. Words, according to this view, obscure reality, which may only be grasped intuitively, in silence or by "direct pointing".

HU'I-NENG: THE SIXTH PATRIARCH

Hu'i-neng, who became the sixth and greatest of the Ch'an patriarchs, was admitted as a boy to a south Chinese monastery c.AD650, where for a time he pounded rice and gathered firewood. When the fifth patriarch was ready to retire, he decided to choose his successor by means of a competition to compose a poem that most perfectly expressed Ch'an doctrine. The following entry, written by a senior monk on a monastery wall, was expected to win:

The body is the tree of wisdom.
The mind is a bright mirror.
Always wipe them diligently.
Let no dust fall on them.

To this the dying patriarch responded: "You have arrived at the door but not entered. It will be futile to seek Perfect Wisdom (*prajna*) with such a view. One must enter the door and see his self-nature." Intuitively comprehending that "self nature" was both "nothing" and "Buddha mind", Hu'i-neng inscribed his own verse on the wall:

Enlightenment is not a tree.
Nor is the mind a mirror.
Since originally there was nothing,
what would the dust fall on?

This famous poem remains a summation of the "emptiness" doctrine as interpreted by Ch'an.

This 10th–13th-century Sung dynasty mural from China portrays Hu'i-neng as though thoughtfully attempting to harmonize acceptance of the patriarchal robe with seclusion or exile. Although Hu'i-neng took the robe, monastic rivalries forced him into retirement until he was almost forty.

"If you should meet the Buddha, kill him," said Ch'an master I-hsuan. "If you should meet the patriarchs or the *arhats* on your way, kill them too ... Bodhidharma was an old bearded barbarian ... *Nirvana* and *bodhi* are dead stumps to tie your donkeys to. The sacred teachings are only lists of ghosts, sheets of paper fit for wiping the pus from your boils." This hilarious iconoclasm comes from the experience of Buddhist emptiness and a cheerful contempt for "lip-service" *dharma*. What joyfully enraged these sages was the ossification – as literature and religion – of the Buddha's intuitive subjectivity. The thrust of Ch'an was to subvert conventional thinking and second-hand knowledge until words such as Buddha, *dharma* and enlightenment regained meaning through personal experience.

Yet the students of these T'ang sages were also subject to a hard discipline. Without Ch'an discipline – sleepless hours of painful meditation, submission to masters – one could not follow Ch'an. But once the student had transcended discipline and perceived its place in the world of relative truth, the mind was freed from mere faith and symbols. Students, like the Buddha, could then see the truth: they became their meditation.

To wake the mind, to shock students from the limits of conventional intelligence, some Ch'an teachers specialized in surprise and conundrum. They set riddles (*kung-ans*), such as "How do you get the goose out of the bottle?" Shouts or blows might greet an answer based on theoretical analysis of ideas. But it was compassion that inspired the Ch'an master. Ch'an is a Mahayana school and the Mahayanist *bodhisattva*'s vow is to lead all beings to enlightenment – although the old Ch'an masters might have ridiculed such formulae.

The first Ch'an patriarch Bodhidharma is depicted here, as often, with a ferocious gaze.

SUCHNESS, THUSNESS

One of the debates within Ch'an circles was on the difference between "*tathagata*" and "patriarch" meditation. The term *tathagata* (thus come or thus gone) is a synonym for the Buddha. *Tathagata* meditation, like the historical Buddha's, has some intellectual content (see the Law of Causality, p.30). Patriarch meditation is purely intuitive. But because the human mind is essentially "Buddha-mind", and Buddha-mind is empty and sublime, the Ch'an practitioner's task was to eliminate thought blocking the mind's perception of mind "as it is": the nature of the human mind's reality as a part of all reality.

Following from this, a discussion arose about "gradual" and "sudden" enlightenment. The path to enlightenment for most Buddhists involved years (or many lives) of study and meditation. Ch'an cut through this. Focusing on non-verbalized meditation experience, the Ch'an practitioner might grasp the absolute in one moment of illumination. This absolute is often described by the Sanskrit term *tathata* (suchness), from the Yogacara school (see p.62). In both sound and meaning this word represents a quasi-non-verbal response to the world in both its unity and multiplicity. A Mahayana story recounts how the Buddha once, instead of delivering a verbal discourse, silently held up a flower. The Buddha's disciple Kashyapa understood the gesture. What Kashyapa saw was *tathata*: the simple, immediate "suchness" of phenomena; of life, mortality and Buddhahood in a casually picked flower with a life of a few hours. Kashyapa's enlightenment – like a silent "Ah!" – was the prototype of Ch'an illumination.

A Chinese sage admiring a waterfall (Fu Baoshi, 1964).

Buddhism in Japan

Buddhism came to Japan from Korea in the 6th century AD and within a generation, helped by its association with Chinese models, the Buddhist *dharma* (doctrine) was proclaimed state religion. To convert the mass of Japanese Shinto devotees was more difficult: but, through a gradual convergence of Buddhism and Shinto, this was achieved by the 8th century. Two great periods of Buddhist activity followed in the successive imperial capitals of Nara and Kyoto. Just as the arts in both cities derived inspiration from China, so Chinese schools of thought were transposed to Japan and given special inflection. Four important schools were established between the 8th and 12th centuries. It was, paradoxically, the rise of the military Shogunate in the 12th century that helped Zen, Japan's most celebrated religious culture, to establish itself.

In the late 19th century, Buddhism and Shinto formally separated and Buddhism declined somewhat. State Shintoism, with its deified emperor, reached a climax in the 1930s, but when this was dismantled in 1945, Buddhism experienced a revival. Post-war uncertainties led to the growth of small Buddhist sects, some offering quick attainment of worldly goals. Perhaps more importantly, philosophers of the Kyoto school have interpreted Zen to the Japanese intelligentsia in a new, modern light.

A Zen temple-garden harmonizing manufactured articles with natural elements. Plants, stones and water conspire to suggest change and impersonality. In this tranquillity the mind both rests and apprehends the "suchness of what is" in its state of becoming.

Shinto: the way of the gods

A Shinto shrine in Hotaka, Japan, where kami *(sacred power) is said to reside.*

Early Shinto devotional practice varied according to region. There was no organized priesthood; instead, people worshipped their local *kamis* at shrines in the charge of mediums who communicated their wishes to the powers. One of the oldest surviving Shinto shrines was dedicated to the sun goddess Amaterasu, the imperial *kami*. The first Japanese emperor was, according to legend, directly descended from Amaterasu. And it was through the charisma of this divine ancestry and the receipt of instructions from the sun goddess who was his family *kami* that the emperor's rule derived its

The earliest religions of the Japanese islands were no doubt similar to the shamanistic cults of northeast Asia and the northern Pacific rim of America. The ancient Japanese who colonized the islands probably brought with them the spiritual beliefs which, much later, became known as Shinto: "the way of *kami* [gods, deities]".

The precise definition of *kami* has long been argued. "Anything outside the ordinary," wrote one Japanese scholar, "with superior power or which was awe-inspiring was called *kami.*" *Kami* – sacred power – is believed to be present in both animate and inanimate things, and might thus reside within great people and ancestors, as well as, not least, in sacred places, rocks, trees and mountains.

A high-ranking Shinto priest in temple precincts with attendants.

EARLY BUDDHISM IN JAPAN

Buddhism first entered Japan from Korea in the 6th century AD – about 1,000 years after the death of the Buddha. Confucian ideas from Han China had been current at the Japanese court since the 5th century AD. By the time Buddhism took root in Japan *c.*AD600, an often mutually tolerant presence of three systems – Shinto, Buddhism and Confucianism – therefore existed. The power behind the establishment of Japanese Buddhism was the imperial regent: a Buddhist convert of enterprise and vision who took the Buddhist name of Shotoku (Wise and Virtuous). Shotoku proclaimed Buddhism as state religion in AD594 and is said to have issued the famous "Seventeen Article Constitution" containing an order to "revere the Three Jewels" of Buddha, *dharma* (doctrine) and *sangha* (religious community).

As the new religion spread, Buddhist temples donated by powerful Japanese clans proliferated. But despite his personal loyalty to the Buddhists, the regent Shotoku ordained government support for a new Shinto priesthood. By the beginning of the 8th century AD a curious synthesis of the two religions had taken place. Because rural Japanese were still devoted to their local *kamis*, the Buddhists, realizing that they could not ignore the support of the masses, opened their temples to Shinto shrines. Conversely, Buddhist altars were allowed near Shinto shrines. A century later, this initial convergence led to Ryobu-Shinto: a Buddhist-Shinto religion which lasted 1,000 years before finally separating.

The Chinese and Korean missionaries who introduced Buddhism brought with them rituals, images and texts from both the Hinayana and the Mahayana schools which had been most successful in China. Of particular influence in Japan were three texts: the *Lotus Sutra* (see p.91), the *Sutra of Golden Light* and the *Benevolent Kings Sutra*. These were sometimes called the *Three Scriptures Protecting the State*. And in this respect it has often been said that the aim of government support for Buddhism was less to achieve the salvation of the people than to make use of religion as an instrument of power and imperial consolidation.

Shinto devotees, like Buddhists, often build shrines in places of beauty and natural power.

SHAMANISTIC BUDDHISM

One of the most popular forms of early Japanese Buddhism was the creation of shamans (*ubasoku-zenji*). These were rural healers and diviners whose traditional role was threatened by the increasing institutionalization of the Buddhist priesthood. The shamans therefore took to Buddhism themselves and, in spite of opposition from government and the orthodox Buddhist clergy, ministered to the physical and spiritual needs of the rural poor, thus keeping alive local beliefs in a synthesis of Buddhism, Shinto and folk religion.

Chinese influence in the Nara period

For most of the 8th century AD, while the Japanese court was centred in Nara and splendid achievements in the arts were being patronized by the elite, the majority of Japanese people lived wretchedly, a prey to the clans who dominated the provinces and whom the Nara executive tried unsuccessfully to control. The 8th century in China was, by contrast, a period of stability and peace, and Chinese Buddhism, like the order of Confucianism, was attractive to the Japanese aristocracy partly because it came from the civilizing culture of the mainland. Everything Chinese – from legal institutions and the Chinese imperial "Mandate of Heaven", to astrology and the theory of yin and yang – was perceived as orderly, superior and therefore useful for the consolidation of Japanese imperial rule.

This kondo *(hall) is the oldest building of the Horyuji temple, which dates from the 7th to 17th centuries encompassing the Nara period.*

The Buddhist schools that were established during the Nara period mostly corresponded to major Chinese schools. Among the Japanese "Six Sects" adopted from Chinese models were the Sanron (Madhyamika, the Chinese "Three Treatises Sect"), Hosso (Yogacara), Kegon (The Flower Garland school) and Tendai (T'ien-t'ai). Besides these Mahayana schools, there were two of the Hinayana persuasion. But although Japanese Buddhism, like the Buddhism of China, was later to become largely Mahayanist, conservative and aristocratic Hinayana schools dominated Buddhist politics in the Nara and later Hieian periods.

So potent was the impact of Buddhism in the 8th century that the emperor, Shomu, declared himself "a servant of the Three Jewels" (Buddha, *dharma*, *sangha*, see p.101) thus virtually abjuring his semi-divine status. When Shomu abdicated to enter a monastery, his heir, Empress Shotoku, appointed an ambitious monk, Dokyo, as her chief minister. The empress, in her turn, abdicated in Dokyo's favour: but the nobility brought him down, thus thwarting – for the first and last time – the creation of a monastic emperor and an "ecclesiastical" state.

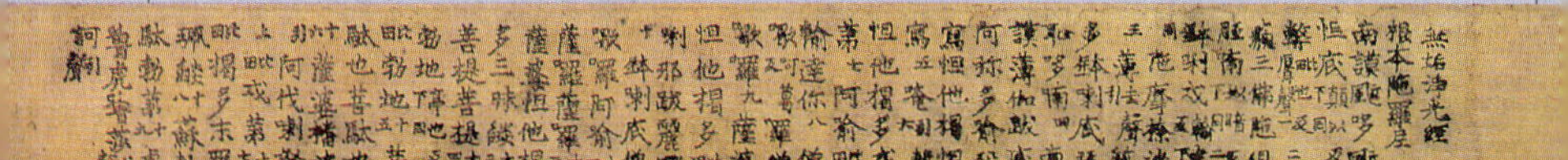

One of the million Buddhist charms that Empress Shotoku had distributed to monasteries between AD764 and 770.

THE MONUMENTAL BUDDHA VAIROCANA

The great wish of Emperor Shomu was to preside over a kingdom that was harmoniously regulated by Buddhist law. A devastating smallpox epidemic in AD735–7 prompted Shomu to establish state-regulated monasteries and convents with large Buddha images in every province. All these monasteries would be under the control of the Great Temple of Todai-ji in Nara. In Todai-ji, the emperor organized the creation of a monumental Buddha, as the "earthly symbol of the Buddha's heavenly tranquillity" which Shomu wished to establish in Japan.

The meditating Vairocana (Cosmic Buddha), over 50 feet (15m) tall, was said to have used 986,180 pounds (450,000kg) of copper; 50,000 carpenters and 370,000 metalsmiths were engaged in its construction. Hills were levelled to provide a site, and the wooden building constructed around it dominated the landscape for miles. Such a spectacle of Buddhist power was, of course, the emperor's intention. In AD749, gold was discovered in Japan. "Hearing this," declared Shomu, "we were astonished and rejoiced." He interpreted the find as a favourable omen, and could now gild the monument with domestic metal. The statue of the Buddha was completed in AD749.

The vast Buddha Hall in Heijokyo (modern-day Nara) has twice been destroyed by fire, and the Great Buddha has been modified many times. But the brush that put the finishing touches to the Buddha's eyes may still be seen in the museum at Nara.

The Great Buddha, much restored, still stands in the hall of Todai-ji temple.

POPULAR SUPPORT FOR THE GREAT BUDDHA PROJECT

The over-taxed Japanese people were at first unwilling to contribute to the expense of creating the Great Buddha (see above). But Emperor Shomu – who had himself taken part in earth-moving for the Todai-ji site – enlisted the support of Gyogi, leader of the shamanistic Buddhists. Taking a Buddhist relic to the shrine of the goddess Amaterasu, Gyogi received a favourable oracle, and travelled around the country convincing people – successfully – that the Shinto deity had given the project her blessing.

Daibutsuden, the hall of the Great Buddha, was originally built with funds that Gyogi helped to raise. It was reconstructed in the 18th century.

Tendai Buddhism

In AD784, the new Hieian emperor abandoned Nara (see pp.102–3), and in AD793 established himself in Kyoto. This move to the "capital of peace and tranquillity" – newly built on the model of the imperial Chinese capital, Chang'an – was motivated partly by a desire to escape monastic politicians in Nara. During the seventh moon of AD788, a young monk called Saicho was climbing Mount Hiei above Kyoto chanting a song: "O Buddhas of complete enlightenment: bless this hut I open on the mountain top!" Like the emperor, Saicho (AD767–822) had left Nara in disgust at the ever more worldly Buddhist establishment there. Saicho's "hut" soon became an important temple which guarded, according to Chinese geomancy, the ill-omened north-east side of Kyoto.

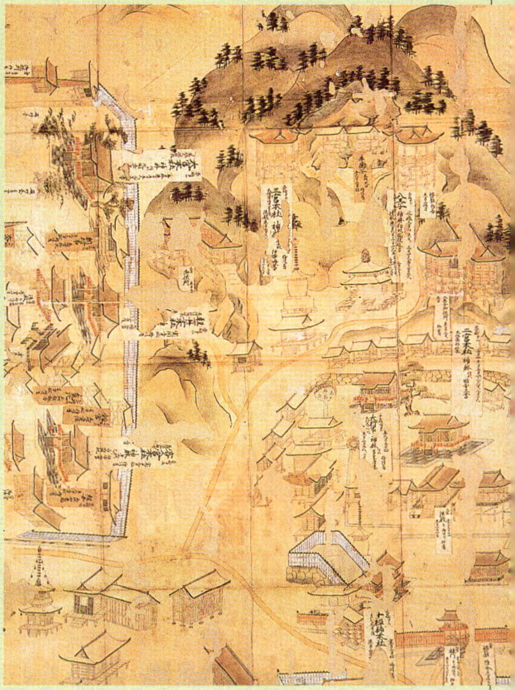

An 18th-century, Edo period map showing the shrines and temples on Mount Hiei.

After a short period in China, where he travelled, unsuccessfully, to seek spiritual sanction for his temple-site, Saicho returned to Mount Hiei and established what would become, with Zen, the largest and most enduring school of Japanese Buddhism. This was Tendai, modelled on the Chinese T'ien-t'ai which based its doctrine on the *Lotus Sutra* (see pp.90–91).

Three main features characterized Saicho's Buddhism. First, it was completely universalist. "All human beings," wrote Saicho, following T'ien-t'ai doctrine, "have the lotus of Buddhahood within them." This was a breakthrough for Japanese Buddhism, for in the Nara period Buddhism had become increasingly the vehicle of a monastic plutocracy or the medium for a high-brow aesthetic. Secondly, Saicho

A modern-day Tendai monk at his devotions in a Kyoto temple.

imposed an unusually strict discipline on his monks. Before leaving Mount Hiei to teach, each monk had to spend twelve years in the monastery, practising concentration and insight (*shikan*). Thirdly, Saicho saw his monastery as the "Centre of Protection of the Nation". Once a monk had trained on Mount Hiei, his role took on a nationalist complexion, expressing – through his *bodhisattva* vow to save souls – a loyalty for "the country of Great Japan". But despite close ties with the emperor in Kyoto, Saicho never received permission to ordain Mahayana monks on Mount Hiei. Until after Saicho's death, Nara was the only sanctioned ordination centre.

A 17th-century woodblock print from a gazetteer for travellers, showing a temple in Kyoto, the centre of Tendai Buddhism.

TENDAI AFTER SAICHO'S DEATH

Saicho's universalist teaching extended throughout the Buddhist and non-Buddhist domains. On the one hand he was vehement in his opposition to elitist Nara doctrine which stressed the need for both doctrinal knowledge and formal practice. On the other hand, he was active in seeking a greater closeness with the Shinto religion. "The King of the Mountain", Shinto's guardian spirit of Mount Hiei, was, for example, an object of Saicho's own veneration. The fusion resulted in the creation of "Mountain-king One-truth", a popular amalgamation of Tendai and Shinto.

After Saicho's death, an immense number of shrines and monastery buildings grew up on Mount Hiei. At Tendai's height, there were probably 3,000 temples on the mountain: but most of these had vanished by the 17th century. As Tendai developed, it incorporated other Buddhist doctrines. The Tendai monk Ennin (AD794–864), for example, travelled to China and returned to add the study of *mandalas* (see p.107) and the cult of *Nembutsu* (the invocation of the Buddha's name) to Tendai practice. Thus, after Saicho's death, Tendai frequently became known as Mikkyo, a branch of "esoteric Buddhism".

In the 11th century, political disputes within Tendai and between Tendai and the Hosso school (Yogacara; see p.62) burst into violence. The monastic factions on Mount Hiei all kept armed priests and mercenaries, who frequently erupted through Kyoto and into one another's temples. The temple of Miidera, a major centre of esoteric Tendai, was burned down twice in the 11th century, and seven more times within the next three centuries. As often as it was burned it was rebuilt. The phenomenon of the warrior monk dominated the medieval period.

Kukai's Shingon school

A group of Shingon monks depicted after an initiation ceremony, from a 17th-century illustrated biography of Kukai. Their "witnesses" are seated in the background.

"His memory lives all over the country, his name is a household word, not only as a saint, but as a preacher, a scholar, a poet, a painter, an inventor, and a great calligrapher." This was Kukai (AD774–835), a Nara aristocrat, a graduate of Nara's Confucian college, and perhaps the most celebrated of all Japanese religious figures; he is said to have written his first treatise, on Confucianism, Taoism and Buddhism, aged seventeen.

Upholding Buddhism as the only truth, but dissatisfied with the doctrines in Japan, Kukai went to China in AD804 in search of a unifying system. Fluent and literate in Chinese, the young monk found favour both at the T'ang court and with the Buddhist master Hui-kuo. Hui-kuo died in AD805, but not before transmitting to Kukai the secret doctrines of Mantrayana (True Words), an esoteric system dependent on personal transmission from master to pupil. Returning to Japan, Kukai, supported by a new emperor, established the Shingon (Mantrayana) school in Kyoto. Shingon, alongside the Tendai school, dominated Japanese Buddhism until the 12th century. And both these schools survived to influence most other forms of Japanese Buddhism.

The name Shingon is from Chinese *chen-yen* (*mantra*, mystic syllable), and the Chinese and Japanese *mantra* schools derive from the Indian Tantra (see pp.134–7). Absolute truth, according to Mantrayana, is realized through the "Three Mysteries" of body, speech and mind. Through repetition of *mantras*, contemplation of *mandalas* (sacred diagrams) and use of ritual gestures (*mudras*), enlightenment might be realized and Buddhahood achieved.

Shingon doctrine was believed to be the teaching not of the historical Buddha Shakyamuni, but of the cosmic Buddha Vairocana – one of five *dhyani* (meditating) or *Jina* (conqueror) Buddhas identified with the *Dharma-kaya*, the ultimate Buddha (see pp.62–3). Shakyamuni delivered a simplified "public" doctrine; Vairocana's teaching was sublime and virtually inexpressible in language. Doctrinally, Shingon has little on which to discourse. The exalted nature of universal truth was simply a vision of Vairocana as symbolized in chosen gestures, *mandalas* and mystic syllables. Kukai insisted on the importance of using Sanskrit: "True words in the original language are exceedingly abstruse, each word possessing a profound meaning. This meaning is changed when its sound is altered. That is why we must go back to the source."

SHINGON *MANDALAS*

The cosmos, according to Shingon, is a manifestation of Vairocana Buddha. This is in two parts: the ultimate, indestructible "diamond" (*vajradhatu*); and the material, perishable, dynamic "womb" (*garbhadhatu*). All reality flows from the communion of these opposites, which is Buddha. But, "in truth," wrote Kukai, "this doctrine is too profound for writing. With the help of painting, however, it may be understood. Art reveals to us the state of perfection." Shingon's greatest art form was the *mandala*. With glowing colours, in which red and blue predominate, the "diamond" is symbolized by a cluster of nine squares. The Womb Mandala is built of concentric squares, at the centre of which is a lotus with a Buddha seated on each of its eight petals, and Vairocana meditating on a central circle. Sanskrit *mantras* are often inscribed on the lotus petals. *Mandala* painters also sometimes use demonic imagery. Many aspects of the world are terrible: but these too "are Buddha" and are believed to have Buddha nature.

A magical diagram or mandala *from 9th-century Dun-huang, brimming with Buddhist symbols of the sort Kukai would have encountered during his studies in China. At the centre is a wheel or a lotus signifying the* dharma.

Pure Land in Japan

Since the Buddha's proclamation of the *dharma* (doctrine) in 6th-century BC India, most Buddhists have been preoccupied with the relationship between suffering and salvation. According to early texts, *nirvana* (enlightenment) was for those who had transcended desire and arrived at an understanding of truth: this experience of "things as they are" was a precondition of *nirvana*. In the 1st century AD, Mahayana Buddhism (see pp.60–63) brought a change of emphasis: salvation without *nirvana* was presented as possible not just for a dharmic elite, but for the mass of people prepared to put faith in a deified Buddha. In 3rd-century AD China, Pure Land, a movement offering salvation in Amitabha's western paradise (see p.92), evolved partly in reaction to the misery following the collapse of the great Han empire. A millennium later, the same Buddhist movement took root in Japan when the Kamakura shoguns wrested power from the Kyoto imperium and initiated a long period of feudalism.

A 17th-century hanging scroll depicting Amida Buddha in the western paradise, surrounded by the faithful listening to him preach.

THE WHITE PATH

A parable of an early Chinese Amidist called Zendo was much celebrated in Japan. It tells of a man who is travelling west but whose journey is halted by an immense plain of water. The only way across is on a narrow white path, which is battered by waves and flames from both sides. The traveller looks back and sees armed bandits and wild animals bearing down on him. The only way forward is on the white path. The moment the man has made a decision to advance, he hears a voice calling, "With right thought and singleness of heart walk on without fear. I will protect you." It is the voice of Amida. The traveller safely walks along the path and reaches Amida's western paradise.

Pure Land had its beginnings in the Hieian period, but it was the monk Honen (AD1133–1212) who took the cult of Amida (Chinese Amitabha; see pp.92–3) to the heart of Japanese Buddhism. Honen started his career as a student of Tendai (see pp.104–5) at the Mount Hiei monastery. Increasingly eclectic, Tendai, in its devotional, ritual and meditational aspects, accommodated most types of Buddhist practice. But after a period of searching, Honen became dissatisfied with Tendai, and became a devotee of Amida. The central difference was the choice between enlightenment or rebirth in a Pure Land (Japanese, *jodo*). Viewing enlightenment as an unlikely prospect for sinful people in a violent age, Honen argued in his lucid *One Sheet of Paper* that *Nembutsu* (repetition of *Namu Amida Butsu*, Homage to Amida) would take the genuinely faithful supplicant to Amida Buddha's paradise. Although Amida is merciful and forgiving, the devotee must cultivate "a sincere, deep-believing and longing heart" with which to recite the *Nembutsu*. Once the desire for *jodo* is established, *Nembutsu* must become "the main work of life".

HONEN'S FOLLOWER SHINRAN

Like his amiable, undogmatic master, Honen's disciple Shinran (AD1173–1262) had no intention of founding a separate school. But Shinran, a man of humility and with a burning sense of his own unworthiness, made significant contributions to Japanese Buddhism. He broadened the prospect of Amidist salvation by claiming that Amida had already forgiven everyone. The *Nembutsu* (see above) was less an appeal to Amida than a prayer of gratitude for his mercy. Shinran, "neither monk nor layman", married and had children, setting a lasting precedent for later Japanese monks.

This Japanese mandala *represents the western paradise as a holy court with Amida Buddha at its centre on a lotus seat.*

Nichiren

The career of Nichiren (AD1222–82) is perhaps the most unusual in Japanese Buddhist history.

"Born a son of the lowest caste," he was destined, in his own view, to become "the pillar of Japan, the eye of the nation". It was Nichiren's ambition that the Japanese state religion should be based on practice derived from the *Lotus Sutra* (see pp.90–91)

Nichiren began as a Tendai monk studying on Mount Hiei. Tendai Buddhism (see pp.104–5) was based on the *Lotus Sutra*, and in many respects Nichiren's doctrine was indistinguishable from Tendai. Two issues isolated Nichiren: the militant style of his self-presentation; and his insistence that the *Lotus* should inform the practice of government. Nichiren made his views public in hotly worded language, attacking both secular and Buddhist establishments. The response was consistently negative, and the vociferous monk was banished to the island of Izu.

There, between 1261 and 1263, "day and night, walking, standing, sitting, lying", Nichiren threw himself into renewed study of the *Lotus*. During this period he became convinced that certain passages in the *Sutra* ("they will deride and abuse us, they will strike us with sticks and stones") were prophetic references to his own persecution.

After his release, Nichiren continued to berate the establishment. It was a violent era; he made enemies easily, and despite later fulfilment of his warning that the Mongols would invade Japan, he was sentenced to death. According to legend, the axe that was raised to behead him was struck by lightning. Nichiren again went into exile. On the island of Sado, he became convinced that he was Visishtacarita (Japanese, Jogyo), a *bodhisattva* "of superb action" named in the *Lotus Sutra*.

This dramatic woodblock print by Kuniyoshi (1797–1861) shows Nichiren calming the sea on his way to exile. The words Namu Myoho-renge-kyo *(Homage to the* Lotus Sutra*) appear auspiciously in the water.*

At the end of his period of exile, Nichiren retired to obscurity at Minobu, where he entered a quieter but no less apocalyptic phase, still dreaming of a unified Buddhist assembly. He likened the Vulture Peak where Buddha Shakyamuni had taught to his own hermitage. "I live in a lonely mountain retreat," he wrote. "But in Nichiren's bosom is secretly enshrined the great mystery which the Lord Shakyamuni transmitted to me. This place being the abode of such a man who has realized

A lavish Japanese ornamental scroll of the Lotus Sutra *dating from the mid-17th century.*

the Lotus of Truth, how can it be less noble than the Vulture Peak?"

Nichiren devised two main vehicles of practice. One was the study of a *mandala* of his own design symbolizing the unified, original Buddha. More important, however, was the repetition of *Namu Myoho-renge-kyo* (Homage to the *Lotus Sutra*). While denouncing as "hell" the Amidists' practice of reciting the *Nembutsu* (see pp.108–9), Nichiren was convinced that the repetition of his formula, even once a year or once in a lifetime, was conducive to salvation, the achievement of Buddhahood.

In response to Westernization in 20th-century Japan and to the fast-changing post-war world, the Nichiren school, divided into a number of subsects, has greatly increased its popularity, attracting followers in Europe and the United States over the last decade.

NICHIREN'S TEACHING

Whereas the Shingon school worshipped the Buddha Vairocana, and the devotees of Pure Land called upon Amida, for Nichiren, there was simply one Buddha, whose forms, as described in the *Lotus Sutra*, were inseparable. In his 1261 exile, Nichiren set down the five elements of his creed. First, the *Lotus Sutra* is the perfect exposition of truth. Second, this age (called Mappo in Buddhist historiography: the final age in a series of increasing degeneration) requires a simple, definite religion. Third, Mappo is the age in which the doctrine should be proclaimed. Fourth, this should be done in Japan, and later universally. Fifth, all other Buddhist systems have done their work; they should yield to the *Lotus* and thus unify religion. "If those who preach false doctrine are suppressed," wrote Nichiren, "and those who hold the true faith are respected, then the country will be at peace."

The beginnings of Zen

Minamoto Yoritomo portrayed on a silk scroll. A 14th-century copy of a 12th-century painting by Takanobu.

Zen came to Japan in the mid-12th century AD, when the Kyoto-based ruling aristocracy finally lost power to the military class of Kamakura. The might of military clans had been rising since the 9th century. In 1156 the Taira clan, who already controlled half of Japan, established a dictatorship in Kamakura, and the emperor was effectively reduced to a puppet. Thirty years later, after terrible wars, the Taira lost to their rivals the Minamoto. In 1192, Minamoto Yoritomo became the first shogun, or "barbarian-subduing supreme general". The shogun system would last until 1868, when power returned to the emperor.

A year before the shogunate was established, the Japanese monk Eisai returned from China, where he had been studying Ch'an Buddhism, and was recognized as a new master. Eisai brought home with him two things: Rinzai Zen Buddhism and tea. Regarded by Eisai as "the most wonderful medicine" and "the secret of long life", tea soon became Japan's national drink. Its preparation by Zen monks would later develop into the exquisite Japanese Tea Ceremony (see p.121).

Zen Buddhism was greeted with less enthusiasm by the Kyoto elite than tea. Tendai, Shingon and Pure Land represented the established practice in the capital and, with their beautiful rituals, these forms of Buddhism had become comfortable to live with. By contrast, the fierce demands of Zen, with its emphasis on personal effort and the promise of enlightenment rather than heaven, seemed rebarbative and disturbing. Furthermore, since Buddhism had become "Japanese", ideas from China were no longer fashionable. Perceiving the fruitlessness of his mission in Kyoto, Eisai moved northeast to Kamakura. Here, paradoxically, the subtleties of Zen found favour with the shogun's down-to-earth warrior caste, the samurai. The warrior monk had long been a feature of Japanese life. The samurai, by contrast, used Zen as a method of concentration and focus.

"Zen" is Japanese for Ch'an, which itself derives from the Sanskrit *dhyana*

The gestures of a Japanese tea master with water ladle appear at once beautifully ritualized and spontaneously unforced.

(meditation). Two main schools of Ch'an Buddhism thrived in Sung dynasty China, both emphasizing meditation and a non-ritualistic, direct contemplation of reality. Eliminating traditional Buddhist learning, Ch'an aimed at "direct pointing to the mind and perceiving one's true nature".

At the basis of Cha'an and Zen philosophy is the Mahayana theory of universal Buddhahood. "Mind" and "one's true nature" are expressions of the idea that all beings are Buddhas, and that "Buddha mind" is the shared medium in which people live (see p.97). Why then should it take years of meditation (*zazen*) to return to the "original mind" which was enlightened all the time? Zen masters claim that this is because we are chronically limited by a belief in the personal self, and the illusion of having this self blinds us to the greater reality, or as Eisai writes, "the highest inner wisdom, the insight of *nirvana*".

THE SAMURAI WARRIOR'S WAY OF THE SWORD

The ethos of the Kamakura regime was one of discipline and frugality, but to many of Kamakura's warriors swordsmanship became primarily a spiritual discipline. The samurai ethic was based on loyalty, filial piety, benevolence and asceticism. This harmonized well with the rigours of Zen training. On a deeper level, the warrior cultivated Zen in action: fearlessness of death and a spontaneity of engagement in which the swordsman moved without conscious control but with almost supernatural precision. To achieve such a condition, the warrior trained to empty himself of ego and intention, and to act, in the face of death, in a condition of "no-mind". This was Zen meditation with "mind on no object".

A Japanese samurai wields his sword in this 19th-century woodblock print.

Rinzai Zen: the study of *koans*

Asked one day if a dog had Buddha nature, Chinese master Chao-chou (Japanese, Joshu) heretically retorted: "*Wu*!" ("Not!" – better known perhaps as the Japanese *Mu*). Replying later to the identical question, but this time affirming Mahayana doctrine, Chao-chou said: "Yes!" – for all beings have Buddha nature.

Joshu's shocking expletive is famous in Zen as one of 1,700 paradoxes and conundrums (*koans*) that are the basis of Rinzai meditation. Meditation on *koans* – most of which, like *Mu*!, are drawn from sayings of old Zen masters – is designed to lead Rinzai students through ever-deepening experiences of "sudden" enlightenment (*satori*). The emphasis is both on long effort and on moments of electrifying vision. To achieve this vision, the student is induced to abandon thought, and in exhaustive dedication to an often overtly meaningless riddle, open him- or herself to a reality that is inexpressible in words and can only be realized through intuition. To be "enlightened" once, to see the truth of a Rinzai *koan*, is a limited, but significant step. Complete for a time, it is only satisfactory if the vision is authenticated by a Rinzai master (*roshi*), and then only if it is extended in pursuit of deeper understanding and more difficult *koans*. There is no "answer" to Joshu's "*Mu*!". The master's very act of negation is a way of demonstrating that Buddhism is not about answers or doctrine. It is easy, teaches Zen, to proclaim a belief, but to comprehend that belief involves travelling far beyond saying "Yes" to it.

The practice of *koan* meditation was developed in China during the T'ang dynasty (see pp.94–5), but its present Japanese form derives from Hakuin (1685–1768), a Zen master who was also a poet and a great artist and calligrapher. Hakuin's own extraordinary account of *koan* meditation is famous in Zen history:

"Joshu's *Mu* was the *koan* given me," writes Hakuin, "and I earnestly applied myself to it. I did not eat or sleep for days and nights, when suddenly a great concentration took place in my mind. I felt as if I were freezing in an ice-field extending thousands of miles, and in myself there was a sense of complete transparency ... I felt like a simpleton and there was nothing in the world but Joshu's *Mu*. I attended lectures but they sounded like a discussion in some distant hall and sometimes I felt as if I were flying through the air. Days passed ... When I suddenly woke I found I was Ganto [an obscure reference to a murdered Zen master] and that through all the changes of time nothing of my personality had been lost. My doubts and indecisions were dissolved like melting ice. I called out 'Wonderful! There is no birth and death from which to escape! There is no supreme knowledge...' "

Hakuin was coldly received in the interview that followed his *satori*. "Rubbish! Rubbish!" his master responded. Some time later, Hakuin stood immersed in thought at the doorway of a woman who had refused him alms. Misinterpreting the monk's stubborn presence, the woman knocked him over with her broom. Zen truth burst on Hakuin's mind. He rushed to his master who intuitively grasped his student's transformation. "Come in!" he shouted. "Now you have it!"

One of the many self-portraits by Hakuin (1685–1768), here shown with a horsehair fly-whisk. The forceful, bounding lines of his garment subtly complement and support the modest, fugitive, self-ironic look emerging from the powerful monastic head.

Soto Zen: Dogen

Of the two main schools of Japanese Zen, Soto was the second to take root. Dogen, its founder, began as a pupil of Eisai, the Rinzai master of the late 12th century (see pp.112–13). Like many thinkers of the medieval period, Dogen (1200–1253) started his career at the Tendai monastery near Kyoto, but transferred, aged fourteen, to Eisai's Zen temple. Eisai died soon after, but the young monk continued to study Zen, journeying to China in 1223. He remained in China until 1227, where, as his writings describe, he experienced many obstacles.

In one candid account Dogen records how, in his attachment to formal meditation, he could not at first understand why Chinese monks should submit to seemingly trivial tasks. He recounts how he met a Chinese *tenzo* (monastic cook) who had come to buy mushrooms. "Sir," said Dogen, "why don't you meditate or study *koans* of ancient masters? Why work so hard as a *tenzo*?" "You seem to be ignorant of the true training and meaning of Buddhism!" the old monk laughed. "At that time," confesses Dogen, "I was unable to understand what he meant."

This story, told against himself, illustrates both the humanity of the future teacher and the character of the Zen that Dogen developed. For perhaps more than any other school, Soto emphasizes the importance of making daily actions – from temple rites to defecation – an expression of Buddhist

Dogen's permanent home became Eihei-ji temple (Temple of Eternal Peace) on the Japanese coast. Eihei-ji remains the largest and most important of Japanese Soto temples. Even the wash-room (below) is conceived with Zen power and decorum. RIGHT *A young monk moves with the pace, mindfulness and obedience required of novices.*

A senior monk stands in the meditation hall with the "stick of compassion", which is used, on request, to smack the meditator's shoulder muscles and awaken his or her mind.

consciousness. Practice, according to Soto, is enlightenment. Just to sit in meditation is enlightenment.

Toward the end of his stay in China, Dogen entered the monastery of Zen master Ju-ching, under whose supervision Dogen intensified his practice of *shikan-taza* (just sitting). One morning he heard the abbot scold a monk who was dozing at his meditation. "*Zazen* [meditation] is the dropping away of body and mind! What can you achieve by simply dozing?" At this moment Dogen himself awoke.

"I have experienced the dropping away of body and mind," he reported. Ju-ching confirmed Dogen's enlightenment and gave him permission to return to Japan. "Stay clear of cities, kings and ministers," he advised. "Make your home in deep mountains, remote valleys, transmitting the essence of Zen – even if only to one true *bodhi-* [enlightenment-] seeker."

Back in Japan, Dogen was disappointed to find Rinzai Zen monks living with "their own furniture, fine clothes and stored-away treasures". Turning from established Zen, he built a meditation hall at Kosho-ji temple, where he started training monks and wrote his *Rules of the New Meditation Hall.* In this text, Dogen communicates his passion as a teacher, and his emphasis on constant effort.

"Imagine your head is on fire," he wrote. "Now is the time to save it."

DOGEN'S VOICE

In his relatively short lifetime Dogen wrote works of major importance both to Zen and to Buddhism in general. These range from short works outlining Soto practice to the *Shobogenzo*, a long, majestic book comprising analytic essays in a visionary prose that ranks with the greatest in world literature. Dogen's genius includes the ability to speak with complete directness. Orthodox to both the Mahayana and Hinayana traditions but ignoring the accumulated Buddhist theorizing of 1,500 years, Dogen urgently restates the *dharma* as though it is entirely new. His voice retains its humane, astringent, astonishingly modern timbre. This lofty, austere monk also had the humour and humility that accompanies intellectual honesty. When the emperor offered him the patriarchal robe, he wrote: "If an old monk here wore the purple *kashaya*, the monkeys and the cranes would laugh at him."

Soto Zen: Dogen's practice

Soto Zen is a school of the Mahayana, but Soto practice, as formulated by Dogen, is virtually identical to that of the historical Buddha, to whom Dogen makes frequent reference.

In *A Universal Recommendation for Zazen* he suggests that "You should pay attention to the fact that even the Buddha Shakyamuni had to practise *zazen* [sitting meditation] for six years. And Bodhidharma [the first Ch'an patriarch; see pp.94–5] had to do *zazen* for nine years in order to transmit the Buddha-mind … If you wish to realize the Buddha's Wisdom, you should begin training immediately."

For monks, like these at Eihei-ji monastery, work is an important part of the daily routine and monastic discipline.

Simple, non-ritualized meditation is the essence of Zen. Just as the Buddha before his enlightenment sat down in the forest without premeditation and was overtaken by a foretaste of *nirvana* (see p.13), so Dogen describes Soto meditation as a completely natural experience. But although wisdom arises spontaneously and "not from outside", it nevertheless comes only to the trainee who has submitted to the teaching of a qualified master. The trainee, he writes, "can be compared to a fine piece of timber, and a true master to a good carpenter". The simile corresponds to the image of the turner in the Hinayana *sutras* (see pp.46–7) and Dogen's writings never stray from the orthodox.

Dogen was himself no stranger to the suffering that prompted the Buddha's enlightenment, and most of his teaching represents a means of achieving an undeluded perception of impermanence and not-self (see pp.28–9). Dogen's position within Mahayana

The Buddha described the perfect site for meditation as "the forest, the root of a tree or a lonely place". There, undistracted by desire and the stimulation of company, meditators would find the tranquillity to study their own bodies, minds and karma. *However, even the Buddha's followers congregated during the rainy season, and today Zen monks meditate together on a daily basis.*

ETHICS AND SAMENESS

Dogen emphasizes the importance of a Buddhist ethic based on the *bodhisattva* vow: "Save others before you realize your own enlightenment." His thought also attempts to remove intellectual antitheses. He meditates on the unity of life and death, being and non-being and the Buddhist doctrine of "sameness".

A Zen caricature of Bodhidharma, whose teaching in the 6th century AD *informed much of Dogen's thought.*

"To study the Way," he writes, "is to study the self. To study the self is to forget the self. To forget the self is to be enlightened by all things. To be thus enlightened is to remove the barriers between one's self and others." In harmony with this are the Four Great Vows of Zen meditation: "Sentient beings are innumerable. I vow to save them. Our passions are inexhaustible. I vow to extinguish them. The holy doctrines cannot be measured. I vow to study them. The path of the Buddhas is hard to reach. I vow to attain it."

PRACTICE SITTING

Dogen wrote detailed instructions for Zen practitioners. Some of these, such as the prohibition against fault-finding in others, are moral, others are in the form of simple rules. Perhaps most enduring are Dogen's guidelines for meditation.

Meditation should be practised in a quiet room, in the lotus posture, with open eyes, loose clothing, an upright back and the breath regulated quietly. Then, Dogen instructs, "Think of non-thinking ... by thinking beyond thinking and non-thinking. This is the basis of *zazen*."

Zen monks in zazen. *Like the first patriarch, they sit with lowered eyes before a blank wall.*

doctrine is likewise unambiguous. "Exert yourself in the Way that points directly to your original [Buddha] nature," he writes. But trying too hard will lead to "clinging" and attachment to the idea of enlightenment. "Setting everything aside," he continues, "think of neither good nor evil, right nor wrong. Thus having stopped the various functions of your mind, give up even the idea of becoming a Buddha."

Although the experience of *satori* (enlightenment) is a feature of Soto Zen, Dogen favoured a gradual progress toward *bodhi*-mind: the mind which has dropped the desire for "fame and profit" and which "sees the flux of arising and decaying".

From the emptiness of not-self, Dogen urges, "simply practise Buddhism for the sake of Buddhism; that is the true Way."

Zen and the arts

Early Zen masters, from Bodhidharma (see pp.94–5) onward, were traditionally opposed to iconography or artistic representation of the Buddha. Since the aim of Zen is to transcend concepts and images, the use of icons would distract the mind from rediscovering the emptiness that is its true nature.

Bodhidharma's patriarchal message was almost brutally realistic. There is no Buddha in the world. There is only Buddha-mind in the human mind. Stories of Zen masters merrily burning Buddhist statues to keep themselves warm reinforce this point of view and underline Zen's most extreme anti-aesthetic position. But in spite of itself, Zen – like every school of Buddhism – generated a vast outpouring of art. The exquisite literary work of Dogen, the first and most ascetic Soto master, is just one example. Almost every field of Japanese creativity has been, and continues to be, infused with the spirit of Zen. The briefest list of major Zen arts must include poetry, Noh drama, ceramics, calligraphy and painting, as well as gardening, flower arrangement, archery, swordsmanship, judo and the tea ceremony.

Eugen Herrigel's *Zen in the Art of Archery* (1953) brilliantly explains to Westerners the possibilities of a conjunction of art and Eastern spiritual values. "The right art" is "purposeless, aimless", and is learnt by letting go and "leaving yourself and everything yours behind you" so that all that remains is a "purposeless tension".

The "artless art" that inspires the "bowless and aimless archer" of Zen archery is expressed in other Buddhist activities by bringing meditation to a physical and aesthetic discipline which transcends self-expression. Losing the self in meditation, the practitioner enters the world's universal "thusness" (*tathata*) and with sharp, bold precision expresses "thusness" without superfluous comment.

A master archer at a Japanese samurai festival. Subject and object converge in no-thought.

Zen artists have always been aware of the hazards of being distracted from a strict dharmic path by aesthetic intoxication. But they also would be familiar with the words of the *Heart Sutra*, the Mahayana text which subsumes the relationship between absolute and relative truth with the words: "Here [in this world], form is emptiness, emptiness is form." And since the 13th century, Zen has given the world some of its most miraculously expressive forms.

This lovely late 19th-century woodblock print conveys the spare refinement of the tea-room. The fashionable women make cha-no-yu *into elegant play, yet the ritual transaction remains harmonious. But with quizzical humour, the artist depicts pungent contrasts, such as the super-civilized women in their sumptuous kimonos against the starkness of the tea-room. On the walls hang scrolls of exalted austerity.*

ZEN GARDENS AND THE ZEN TEA CEREMONY

The meeting of "form and emptiness" in Zen creativity finds its clearest expression in the simplest and most natural forms. The Japanese people, since the beginnings of the Shinto tradition (see pp.100–101), have always revered nature, and the Zen expression of this consists either of simply pointing to natural beauty or of creating gardens of exquisitely artificial simplicity.

One example of this is in the garden of the Tenru-ji temple northeast of Kyoto, established in the mid-13th century AD. There, an artist – perhaps invited from Sung China – created a craggy landscape of rocks in the middle of a pond. This grouping of natural forms placed in a harmoniously assymetrical arrangement epitomizes the Zen vision of changeful nature in its original "thusness": simultaneously perfect and yet naturally not "finished".

The Zen tea ceremony (*cha-no-yu*) is traditionally held in such gardens. In spirit, the ceremony embodies principles of harmony, reverence and tranquillity. In practice, the guest walks to the tea hut through a garden where running water and rocks are introduced to symbolize impermanence and not-self. The tea hut is utterly simple. Inside, following complicated etiquette, the host prepares tea with utensils at once refined and ruggedly naive. The silence of the hut, intensified by tiny sounds of fire and water, signifies – perhaps is – the peace of *nirvana*.

A dry Zen garden that has been raked to evoke water. Heaps of sand imply rocky islands. Immaculately patterned, such gardens suggest, with artful simplicity, convergent opposites: matter and emptiness, impermanence and no-time, relative and absolute. Monks have raked the garden with Zen precision.

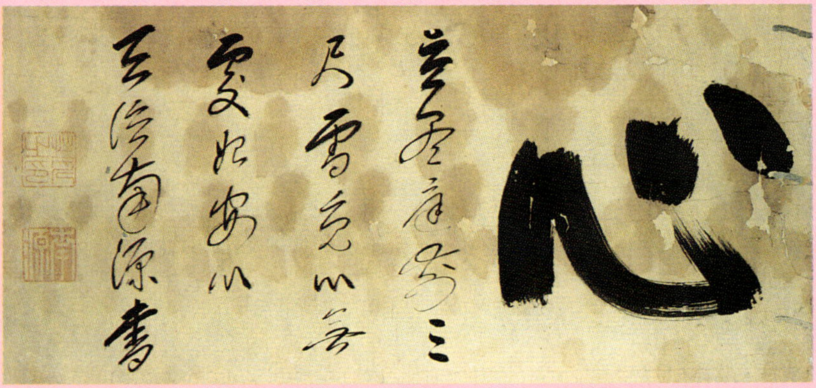

This 17th-century Japanese painting shows how relaxed Zen spontaneity can lead to unconventional script.

In the earliest period of Japanese Buddhism, poetry, song and religious culture were transmitted orally. But by the 6th century AD, Buddhist texts were being transcribed by Japanese monks – although still in Chinese. The conversion of the Japanese language into Chinese characters occurred about a century later, and by the 9th century in Kyoto calligraphy had become an art taken to exalted aesthetic standards both by the Hieian literati and by Buddhist monks.

The first Buddhist leader actively to encourage the use of art for the communication of the *dharma* (doctrine) was the Shingon master Kukai: himself famous as a calligrapher (see pp.106–7). Writing of Zen calligraphy in the 18th century, the great Rinzai master Hakuin referred to the "overwhelming force of enlightened vision" which must inform any work of spiritual and aesthetic worth. Hakuin was himself heir to a tradition which originated at Tenru-ji monastery, where the Zen monk Ikkyu (1394–1481) broke from Hieian convention to create a Zen calligraphy that was rugged, spontaneous and as deceptively casual as the pattern of rocks in the famous Tenru-ji garden. Using fast, bold, often energetically "dry" brush-strokes, Ikkyu shunned the elegance of Hieian brush-work to produce scrolls of vital, stark immediacy.

Calligraphic scrolls were soon put to use as teaching devices or as objects of contemplation. Devotees of the tea ceremony hung scrolls in their tea huts. The brush-strokes conveying a Zen scroll's message are, of course, no mere vehicle: medium and meaning having become inseparable components.

Zen calligraphy has also developed into a meditation in its own right. Deep concentration, insight and spiritual freedom are all found in the simplest strokes of the Zen masters. *Iichi*, a single horizontal line representing "one", or the Zen circle (*enso*) signifying emptiness, as painted by Hakuin, are, for all their simplicity, gestures of spontaneous perfection which derive from years of thought and practice.

ZEN PAINTING

Zen calligraphy and painting share the same unstudied and minimally representational style. But there is a limit to what Zen painters might be expected to produce; everything from their hands must express Buddhist conviction: and the intensity of this depends on the quality of their insight.

One major genre – derived from Chinese landscape painting – focuses on natural scenes. These show vigorously alive grasses, rocks, trees, water, sparsely brushed in mistily washed light or isolated in the whiteness of infinite *nirvanic* space. Then there are studies of flowers or fruit, such as master Mu-ch'i's *Persimmons*, where the sharply observed reality of things is briskly conveyed as ordinary yet sublime.

Also important were the portraits and self-portraits of Zen masters. These, sometimes grotesquely sketched in a severely limited number of strokes, set out to convey the wisdom or authority of their subjects rather than physical likeness. Portraits of the first Zen patriarch Bodhidharma (Japanese, Daruma) show a deformed old monk with vast eyes staring in fierce contemplation. The venerable Hakuin drew portraits of himself in the same exaggerated serio-comic idiom (see p.115).

In a lighter vein are sketches of drunken, carefree hermit clowns such as Han Shan and Shih-te. The two Chinese sages laugh in their cups and sleep in the open. Transcending convention, joyfully expressing a quasi-Taoist *dharma*, they burlesque good form and mock properly sanctioned monastic enlightenment.

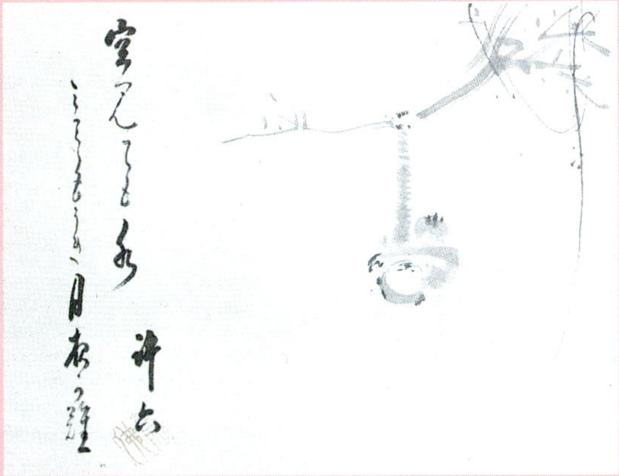

Running script by Matsuo Basho, the greatest of the haiku poets, with a painting by one of his pupils.

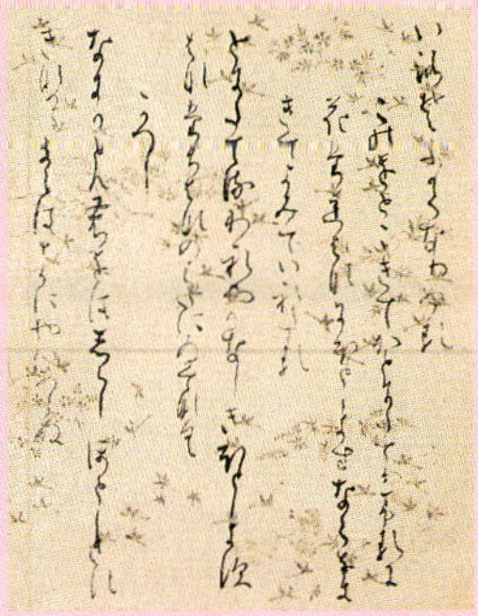

A message from Basho, written two days before his death, apologizing to his pupils for dying before them.

HAIKU

Zen master Rinzai said: "The pure light of each instant of thought is the *dharma-kaya* Buddha within your own house." Haiku is the poetic expression of Zen "instants of thought". Using seventeen syllables and in a splinter of illuminated time, the haiku "points directly" to the wholeness of a perception, then fades from existence. A haiku poem must refer to one of the four seasons – often just suggested through symbols or imagery – but it must also transcend time. It is written from the point of view of the object: the writer's art and, perhaps more importantly, the writer's ego must be imperceptible.

An old pond. Ah!
A frog jumps in.
The splash of water.

Matsuo Basho (1644–94)

Buddhism in Tibet

Tibet was the last of the Asian nations to be reached by Indian missionaries. Helped by the central monarchy, the conversion of the Tibetan people was relatively rapid and thorough. But Bon, the indigenous Tibetan religion, did not die out altogether, and a number of aspects of Bon were absorbed into the Buddhist *dharma* (doctrine). Hinayana and Mahayana travelled across the Himalayas to the "Land of Snows", but it was Mahayana and the Indian Tantra that survived. Both contained a rich infusion of Hindu deism, and were creatively developed by Tibetans into the "completed *dharma*" of the "Diamond Vehicle" (Vajrayana).

The many Tibetan monastic schools differed in details of ritual and practice, but were united in their orthodoxy, which was underpinned by the heroic project of translating the entire Buddhist canon into Tibetan; many Buddhist Sanskrit texts now only survive in Tibetan translation. A huge and original tradition of Buddhist painting, metalwork and architecture also grew up in the monasteries. Much has been destroyed or desecrated since the Chinese Cultural Revolution in the 1950s; and while some of the barbarities of this have, since 1980, been admitted and to some extent remedied, Tibet remains an occupied country, with a government in exile and most of its leaders in India and the West.

Gyantse Dzong, the administrative centre of the Tibetan province, Tsang. Damaged by British action in 1904 and vandalized in 1959 during the Chinese Cultural Revolution, it has now been restored. The important inner Buddhist sanctuary remains unharmed.

Pre-Buddhist Tibet and the Bon religion

Buddhism first came to Tibet around AD650. Before the arrival of missionary monks, a native religion known as Bon (pronounced "bern") was practised in two main forms. One was a priestly religion which served the early Tibetan kings. Because the kings were sacred rulers and their funeral rites vitally important, the Bon priests' prime responsibility was the continuity of rituals that underpinned the monarchy. The other form of Bon was a shamanistic religion based in rural communities. The shamans were religious adepts whose skills lay in the control of local deities and spirits, many of them malignant, which in huge numbers were believed to haunt every part of Tibet. Using their mastery of trance, spirit-possession and spirit-flight, most shamans of northeast Asia have traditionally empowered their rites with dance, song, drumming and personal amulets. Since misfortune was usually attributed to spirits, it was the shaman's craft, through ritual and magic, to bend these powers to healing, divination and the protection of communities.

Tibet was the last of the great Asian kingdoms to convert to Buddhism. Remote as it appears behind the Himalayan barrier, the "Land of Snows" was once a great power in Asia; between the 7th and 9th centuries AD Tibetan armies pushed far into China, even taking control for a short while of the Chinese capital, Chang'an. Contact with China, Kashmir, India and Nepal during these centuries fed both Buddhist and Hindu ideas into Tibet, and this helped shape the peculiarly rich texture of Tibetan Buddhism.

Rongbuk monastery in the pass six miles (10km) north of Mount Everest base camp.

This 16th–17th-century gilt bronze statue depicts Avalokiteshvara, protective bodhisattva *of Tibet and Nepal.*

BUDDHISM ENTERS TIBET

The early history of Tibetan Buddhism is conventionally divided into two periods. "The First Introduction of the Dharma" starts with King Srong-btsan (died AD650). Unifying Tibet through an unprecedented alliance of warring nobles, Srong-btsan pursued a policy of military expansion. Legend speaks of the influence of two of Srong-btsan's wives – from China and Nepal – who encouraged the king to tolerate the importation of Buddhism to Tibet. Srong-btsan perhaps grasped the unifying potential of Buddhism, and although he probably remained a Bon religionist, he was later canonized – as the first "Buddhist" king – as an incarnation of the *bodhisattva* Avalokiteshvara (see pp.62, 64–5). During the reign of Srong-btsan and his successors, the foundations of Tibetan monastic tradition were laid by monks from India and central Asia; a Tibetan alphabet was adapted from a north Indian script so that translated texts could be written down; and kings, eager to escape the power of Bon priests, enthusiastically supported the Buddhist *dharma.*

It was Khri-srong (AD740–798), the second "*dharma* king", who established the authority of the Buddhist *sangha* (community), and with the arrival in Tibet of the Tantric adept Padmasambhava, the great monastery at Samye was consecrated. There, from *c.*779 onward, Tibetan monks could for the first time be ordained.

The next century saw national disunity and a revival of the Bon religion at the expense of Buddhism.

This period was followed by "The Second Introduction of the Dharma" under King Ye-shes-'od, when surviving monasteries were purged of heretical practice and new monasteries established that were regulated by the Theravada discipline set down in the *Vinaya* (see p.71).

The greatest reformer was the Indian monk Atisha (AD982–1054), who arrived in 1024 and introduced the cult of Avalokiteshvara. Atisha's reforms were reinforced in the 11th century by adepts bringing texts and doctrines from India. Around AD792 a debate at Samye monastery between Indian and Chinese Mahayanists established the Indian school of "gradual enlightenment" as Tibetan orthodoxy; in the 11th century Tantric doctrines finally took hold as well, helping to forge a unified creed in Tibet based on continuing contact with Indian Buddhists.

A 17th–18th-century gilt-bronze statue of Padmasambhava, who brought Tantric practice to Tibet.

Monks and *lamas*

Young Tibetan novices watching the colourful Paro festival.

Buddhism informs virtually every sphere of Tibetan people's lives, but not every religious specialist is required to take monastic orders. Some of the greatest Tibetan *lamas* (teachers), such as Marpa and Milares-pa in the 11th and 12th centuries, have been laymen, and many non-monastic or partially ordained adepts lived in remote hermitages, studying, teaching, practising Tantric rites and meditation. In the course of their training young monks might spend up to three years in a hermitage run by a non-monastic *lama*.

Like most Buddhist monks, fully ordained Tibetan clergy follow the discipline of the *Vinaya* set out in Hinayana scripture (see p.71). The equivalent Mahayana *Vinaya* became the basis of a further mass of native Tibetan rules which governed a studious and ritualistic monastic routine. In 19th-century Tibet, about one sixth of the male population were monks, and as monks had supreme status in all spheres of life, many families tried to offer at least one son for ordination.

A boy probationer can expect to spend three years absorbing the monastic routine, learning to read and write and to recite short texts. A programme of rigorous instruction by *lamas* then starts, each *lama* specializing in *Sutras*, *Vinaya*, *Abhidharma*, medicine or Tantra; these courses are followed by demanding exams. Exercises in competitive public debate devised to train novices in the expression of the "true and innermost essence of the *dharma* [doctrine]" are another feature of Tibetan monastic training.

After twelve years, during which they will have studied and memorized vast numbers of Mahayana texts and commentaries, novices – at the minimum age of twenty – may receive full ordination, and those who shine in their final exams move on for high positions in the academic or political hierarchy.

Monks constructing a festival mandala *with sand and the dust of precious stones. After the festival, the* mandala *will be destroyed, thus expressing the insubstantiality of visible forms.*

MONASTIC ROUTINE

To become a Tibetan monk is to take the *bodhisattva* vow, as expressed in the *Diamond Sutra*, to "lead all beings to *nirvana*". The *bodhisattva*'s exemplary refusal to enter *nirvana* is taken literally: many high monks are believed to be reincarnated *bodhisattvas*, both human and celestial.

The life of a monk is austere and demanding. In the isolation of their cells, monks will meditate, perform prostrations and repeat *mantras* and formulae such as the "Triple Jewel" (see p.41) many thousands of times a day. Communal life involves daily convocations – accompanied by music from conch-shells, drums, bells, gongs, horns and cymbals – for chanting, ritual, the construction of *mandalas* and the organization of complex annual ceremonials.

Beyond their purely religious routines, monks have duties appropriate to their intellectual and spiritual levels both inside and outside the monastery. Tibetan monks, unlike those in the Hinayana tradition, are allowed to work in trade and agriculture; many specialize in secular and religious handcraft. Although monasteries are no longer land-owning institutions, monks pursue administrative careers which they combine with a pastoral role in isolated communities. At the highest level of secular activity is the national and international business on which the welfare of the *sangha* (religious community) and the country depends. Everything from border negotiations to the exercise of civil and criminal justice has been conducted by monks since the 11th century.

Young monks study the Kanjur, *the core Buddhist canon, translated into Tibetan.*

Apart from the meditation that is a Buddhist monk's means of personal salvation and the teaching that is their vehicle of altruistic care, a major focus of the Tibetan *sangha* is the creation and preservation of Tibetan Buddhist culture. Copying, editing, translating and restoring texts are activities of great spiritual merit, as is the construction of devotional images and the creation of *thankas* (paintings on cloth) which are among the chief glories of Tibetan art.

Tibetan monastic schools

All of the twelve or thirteen Tibetan monastic schools derived their practice from the same north Indian Mahayana Mulasarvastivadin sect. Variation between Tibetan sects was therefore largely confined to differing rituals and monastic lineage. Some monasteries were headed by families who maintained power within their own kin groups. Others, with no aristocratic support, controlled hierarchical succession by installing child abbots said to be reincarnations of deceased *lamas*.

In AD1056, Lama Atisha's (see p.127) leading disciple established the Kadam-pa sect. Monastic discipline in the century before Atisha had been in disarray: a magical, quasi-shamanistic Tantra (see pp.134–7) was commonly being practised. Kadam-pa reformed itself to strict *Vinaya* orthodoxy (see p.71). Another sect was established in the same period by Marpa (1012–96) who, like many Tibetan masters, underwent years of study and initiation in India. Marpa studied with Naropa, a Tantric master from Bihar, and returned to found the Kargyu-pa lineage. A layman, Marpa was a working farmer who combined a householder's married life with teaching deep Tantric mysticism and the translation of important Sanskrit texts. Kargyu-pa, his lineage, means "follower of the successive orders": the name implies that each master was initiated and inspired by a previous guru. Naropa, for example, directly followed Tilopa, who was said to have been instructed by the Buddha Vajradhara (see p.141).

This 17th-century Tibetan statue shows Milares-pa, famous for his command of mystical heat, in the thin robe he wore in winter.

Milares-pa (1040–1123), a hermit yogi who started his career as a celebrated and feared magician, was Marpa's chief disciple. His devotional singing helped establish a tradition of Tibetan Buddhist poetry.

THE FIRST DALAI LAMAS

Two separate theories of reincarnation explain the Dalai Lama's spiritual identity. The first is that the deceased *lama*'s spirit is reborn in a child. The chosen baby is enthroned and later initiated and trained as a Ge-lugs-pa monk before he takes office. This notion of reincarnation differs from older Buddhist theory which teaches that rebirth is determined by personal karmic elements. The second theory, that each Dalai Lama is an incarnation of Avalokiteshvara, probably originated in the 17th century. Since Tibet's first "*dharma* king" (see p.127) was also thought to be an incarnation of Avalokiteshvara, the connection suggested between each Dalai Lama and Tibet's first Buddhist benefactor is a powerful one.

His Holiness the fourteenth Dalai Lama.

SA-SKYA-PA, GE-LUGS-PA AND THE DALAI LAMA

The Sa-skya-pa and Ge-lugs-pa schools have both played significant roles in Tibetan history. In AD1244, the abbot of Sa-skya-pa became "prince regent" of Tibet under the protection of the reigning Mongol *khan* (ruler). Later that century, the emperor Kublai Khan buttressed Mongol patronage of Sa-skya-pa's priestly rule. From that time on, until the Chinese repression of Buddhism in Tibet in the 1950s, the country was governed by a hierarchy of *lamas*.

But power eventually flowed to another school. In the early 15th century the Kadam-pa (Yellow Hat) sect evolved into the school called Ge-lugs-pa (Virtuous Style).

The fully restored throne room at Norbu Lingka, the Dalai Lama's former summer residence in Tibet.

Based in Lhasa, Ge-lugs-pa strove for dominance over rival monastic houses. It was not until 1656, again with Mongol support, that the Yellow Hats, led by the fifth Dalai Lama (1617–82), won their struggle. The title Dalai (Ocean of Wisdom) Lama was bestowed by the Mongols. Priest-king of Tibet, the fifth Dalai Lama was proclaimed to be an incarnation of the *bodhisattva* Avalokiteshvara (see p.62). To mark his pre-eminence, the fifth Dalai Lama built a monastic palace on the Red Hill overlooking Lhasa, naming it Potala after Avalokiteshvara's mythical mountain in India.

The Potala Palace, spared the worst of the Chinese Cultural Revolution, is now a state museum.

The Buddhist cosmos

The Adi Buddha Vajrasattva, "primordial Buddha whose essence is the diamond or thunderbolt", worshipped in Tibet and Nepal.

As the Buddha walked to the place where he would die, he remarked to Ananda, "How beautiful is Jambu-dvipa [rose-apple island]!" As well as simply meaning "India", the Buddha was alluding to a particular cosmic sphere. In Tibetan Buddhist cosmology, which owes much to Hindu-Buddhist myth, Jambu-dvipa refers to the human continent, one of four that surround Mount Meru, the cosmic axis. The universe (*loka*) in Hinayana tradition comprises three spheres of existence:

The first is the World of the Senses (*kama-loka*), which includes the following spheres in descending order: six lower heavens; the human world; the demon or titan world; the animal world; the hungry ghost world; the hells. In the lower heavens, such as Tushita (Heaven of Pleasure) and Tavatimsa (Heaven of the Thirty-three Gods), dwell Indra and other Hindu-Buddhist deities. The titans (*asuras*) are semi-divine beings who, according to Hindu tradition, are in perpetual con-

THE BUDDHIST HELLS

Many *lamas* teach that hell is a product of the imagination and, like all human ideas, just an illusory metaphor. But both Hinayana and Mahayana provide detailed and vivid pictures of a number of hells. These infernos lie deep in the earth presided over by the god Yama, who judges the deeds of souls in their last incarnation. The notion of personal responsibility is central to that of expiation. "These your evil deeds," says Yama, "are not the work of your parents or friends. You alone have done them. You alone must gather the fruit." The retribution that follows bad personal *karma* is graphically illustrated by descriptions of torment "in seas of blood and burning coals ... until the last residue of guilt has been expiated".

Hinayana tradition lists eight hells; Tibetan texts enumerate sixteen hot and cold hells. Avici (Endless Torture) is for those who scorned the Buddha or the *sangha* (community). The souls of the unkind and ungenerous, who wander in the sphere above the hells, become hungry ghosts (*pretas*) whose ravenous but tiny mouths take in tormentingly small amounts.

This 20th-century Tibetan Wheel of Becoming shows hell among the six "ways" of rebirth.

flict with the gods over the "great wishing tree" halfway up Mount Meru. There are six "ways" of rebirth available to all beings. None of these is preferable to *nirvana*, but, in descending order, rebirth is possible in the realm of gods, titans, humans, beasts, hungry ghosts and hell.

The second is the Fine-material World (*rupa-loka*) of higher deities.

The third is the Immaterial World (*arupa-loka*), where heavenly beings of the spheres of unbounded space and consciousness dwell.

All those who have experienced nothingness, unbounded space and unbounded consciousness by practising concentrative meditation may be reborn in the last two.

A development of Indian Mahayana that influenced Tibetan Buddhism was the "Vehicle of the Thunderbolt" (Vajrayana, see pp.138–9). According to Vajrayana, there are two further heavens. In the highest realm dwells the Adi Buddha (primal, supreme Buddha) from whose meditation arose five "conqueror" Buddhas (*Jinas*), in the realm below him. *Jinas* are the four Buddhas of the cardinal directions, with Buddha Vairocana in the middle. *Bodhisattvas* such as Avalokiteshvara, Manjushri and Samantabhadra also dwell in the *Jina* heavens as emanations of Buddhas.

Tantric Buddhism

Tantric Buddhism developed in India, but was taken up by the Tibetans in their enthusiastic embrace of the many different forms of Buddhism that crossed the Himalayas. Although it is, therefore, rooted in Indian Buddhism, Tantra's main importance lies in its position as a central part of the complex, eclectic *dharma* (doctrine) that evolved in Tibet and other Himalayan regions. A knowledge of Tantric beliefs and practices is essential to an understanding of the Tibetan *dharma*.

An 18th-century Indian painting showing Kali subduing her husband Shiva. The "terrible" deities of Tantric Buddhism derive from the Hindu notion that gods may have both creative and destructive aspects.

Tantra, a mystical form of Buddhism deriving from a convergence of Buddhist and Hindu ideas, emerged in India around AD700, a thousand years after the Buddha's death. It is easy to represent the teachings that sprang from the Buddha's enlightenment simply as a rational, psychologically introspective system; but the Buddha's teaching was not disengaged from the magico-religious beliefs of his time. In the millennium after his death, Buddhism and Hinduism developed side by side. Hinduism, with its broad embrace, often assimilated Buddhist ideas; the process also went the other way. In Mahayana Buddhism (see pp.60–63), deities and ideas about heaven came from Hinduism; Tantra added popular magico-religious idioms, such as spirits, spells and folkloristic cosmologies, to the Mahayana devotional system.

Shiva and his consort Parvati, important figures in Tantra, from the Elephanta caves, Bombay.

An image central to Tantra is that of male and female deities in generative, sexual union. The male gods of the Hindu pantheon all had female consorts. Especially important to the Hindu Tantra were the figures of Shiva, Lord of Yoga, and his wife, the beautiful and feminine Parvati. But in other manifestations, Parvati was the warrior deity Durga; or the black goddess Kali, who could, in turns, be motherly and destructive. The evolution of Tantra seems to have accompanied a growth in

the importance of such goddesses, from whom, as a divine force, the whole universe was said to come. The symbolism of coupled male and female deities had two main aspects: sexual union suggested the generation of life – biological, material and spiritual. And whereas a male deity might be remote and transcendent, his female partner was thought to be active and accessible – the male god's *shakti* (power, energy) at play in the world of humans.

In association with these symbols there developed sexual rites where men and women, in sexual ecstasy, became male and female deities. But because Tantric theory, like the Mahayana, insists that *samsara* (the cycle of rebirth) and *nirvana* (enlightenment) are one and the same thing, no release from samsaric suffering is sought. Religious devotion is a question of identifying in ever more profound bliss, of which sex is but one aspect, with the play of divine *shakti*.

THE FIVE FORBIDDEN THINGS

Originally, Tantric rites were held in secret because only those who had been initiated into their symbolism could understand their meaning. Tantric adepts met at night, often in a house or temple, but sometimes in a cemetery surrounded by corpses. And because all beings and things are simply an expression of the divine, no caste distinctions were recognized. A Tantric circle might thus have included *brahmins* and "untouchables", all equal in the oneness of *shakti* (divine female energy). To underline this non-dualism, an evening's *puja* (worship) might have been followed by activities taboo to orthodox Hindus: indulgence in alcohol, meat, fish and illicit intercourse. The Sanskrit for each begins with an "m", as does *mudra* (symbolic gesture). *Mudras* are, mysteriously, forbidden neither to Hindus nor to Buddhists. The five "M"s are introduced, not in the spirit of subversion, but as an affirmation of the holiness of all forms and beings.

A sacred erotic carving from a temple complex at Khajuraho, Madhya Pradesh: lovers are opposites converging into sublime unity.

An 18th-century Tibetan bronze showing the Adi (primordial) Buddha with his shakti *(female counterpart).*

The Tantric ideas that entered first the Indian and then the Tibetan *dharma* were not introduced by orthodox monastics. Like its Hindu counterpart, the Buddhist Tantra was the creation of devotees who were isolated from mainstream monastic communities. It was such recluses and lay devotees, outside conventional society, who sought the power that would transform them into Buddhas.

The Tantra is concerned with the integration of ideas often seen as incompatible. And in itself Tantra embraces apparently contradictory elements. The first of these are rituals, spells and belief in spirits which ordinarily belong to folk religion. The second is a body of abstruse texts called *Tantras*. These treatises, usually written in unambiguous Sanskrit, were coded so as to be intelligible only to the initiates surrounding a Tantric guru. Unlike the *Sutras* which expound doctrine, or the *Vinaya* and *Abhidharma* which deal with monastic discipline and theories of knowledge (see p.71), most *Tantras* provide details of *mantras* (mystic syllables), *mudras* (ritual gestures), magical diagrams (*yantras* and *mandalas*) and rites that will transfigure devotees from their secular selves into *siddhas* (individuals of power). Monastic practitioners accept that they will struggle through many lifetimes before reaching *nirvana*; but Tantric adepts believe that with ritual and initiation into arcane realms, they can arrive, through quasi-magical transformation, at Buddhahood. Such beliefs were absorbed and adapted by Tibetan adepts of the Tantra.

MANTRAS

To sing, chant and repeat magic syllables for the conjuring of power has always been in the repertoire of ancient societies. Tribal hunters sing magical songs to heal, to change the weather, to bring animals close to them. Hindu ceremonies are traditionally accompanied by the recitation of *mantras* (auspicious verbal formulae) sometimes taken from the Vedic books. One theory maintains that the whole universe is composed of sound, and that *om*, the greatest of the *mantras*, both evokes all reality and brings the adept into the direct experience of the divine.

Tantric Buddhists adopted many Hindu *mantras* and devised many of their own. The great *mantra* of Tantrism is *Om mani padme hum*. Literally, this means "O jewel in the lotus!" There are several ways of interpreting this. On one level, jewel and lotus are *dharma* and Buddha. On another, jewel and lotus refer to the sacred intercourse of the Buddha and his *shakti*, or Avalokiteshvara with Tara. While *mani* (jewel) and *padme* (in the lotus) are Sanskrit words in grammatical relationship, *om* and *hum* are syllables whose meaning can not be translated. The six syllables of the *mantra* correspond to the six perfections of a *bodhisattva* (see p.62).

A Tibetan gouache depicting the paradise of the Green Tara. The deity Tara was said to have risen from a tear of the bodhisattva *Avalokiteshvara; her sign is the blue lotus. At her feet dancers and musicians gather purified souls for rebirth in the opening lotus of Tara's compassion.*

SHAKTI

Just as the male gods in the Hindu pantheon had spiritual and sexual partners, so, once established in Mahayana as divine beings, the Buddha and *bodhisattvas* acquired female consorts. As the male divinity remained aloof from humanity, it was usually his female partner (*shakti*) who could be invoked to intervene in human affairs. There was a class of Buddhist *shakti* called Tara (female saviour). The Buddha's own *shakti* was sometimes depicted as the goddess Prajnaparamita (see p.65). Like their Hindu counterparts, Buddhas and *bodhisattvas* were often depicted in sexual embrace with a Tara or *shakti*. One meaning of this symbol is that things and ideas the world treats as opposite – male/female, light/darkness, good/evil, *samsara/nirvana* – exist in a state of dynamic tension which the Tantric adept must, through superior knowledge, integrate. The Buddhist Tantra, like many schools of Hindu thought, proclaims that ultimate reality (symbolized in the Tantric embrace) is indivisible.

Vajrayana

The Buddhism of Tibet, or Vajrayana, is often described as the "completed *dharma*", because it absorbed the doctrines of both Hinayana and Mahayana and also embraced north Indian Tantra. Vajrayana monastic training, which involves the study of Hinayana and Mahayana as well as the Buddhist Tantra, is correspondingly "complete". A Vajrayana monk's education, taking him through the entire philosophy, theology and epistemology of Buddhism, is exceptionally long and thorough. Those who reach the level of Vajra master or the academic rank of *geshe* or *rabjam-pa* (overflowingly learned) will have completed twenty or thirty years of study beyond the twelve years prior to ordination.

The vast learning of such *lamas* earns them positions as monastic abbots or formerly, in the Dalai Lama's Ge-lugs-pa school (see p.131), senior positions in the Potala. But these honours are external. Scholarship is valued for its spiritual content and for the purpose of transmitting the Buddhist doctrine to pupils. As in the relationship between Hinduism's Upanishadic gurus and the pupils to whom they taught their "forest wisdom", the Tibetan tradition stresses the supreme importance of personal transmission from master (*rinpoche*, "precious one") to disciple. Also, much Tantric knowledge can only be communicated to students who are being initiated into esoteric doctrine.

Much of this esoteric material comprises the *mantras*, *mudras* and *mandalas* chosen by the master to suit the initiate's particular needs and character. Also of vital importance is the teacher's choice of a tutelary deity for his student. This will be an aspect of a celestial Buddha, *bodhisattva* or Tantric deity whose power will help integrate the students' energies and lead them toward enlightenment (see pp.140–41).

This magnificent Tibetan mandala *shows the deity Hevajra with sixteen arms embracing his consort Nairatmya.*

THE *VAJRA* SYMBOL

In Hindu iconography, the *vajra* of "Vajrayana" was the adamantine, or "diamond-hard", thunderbolt with which Indra, chief of the Vedic gods, made war on the Titans. Transformed from the Hindu image of victorious, indestructible weapon, the *vajra* in the Buddhist Tantra becomes a symbol of ultimate reality. Like the Buddhist wheel, the *vajra*, with its sceptre shape, has royal connotations. But it is the *vajra*'s eternal indestructibility and its combination of solid form and inner space which is interesting to the Buddhist. The *vajra* is also a symbol of male, compassionate, "skilful means" in the search for *nirvana*. Accompanying the *vajra* in many rituals is a bell symbolizing female "perfected knowledge" (*prajnaparamita*). Like many Tantric symbols, male and female make a harmonized duality whose essence is One.

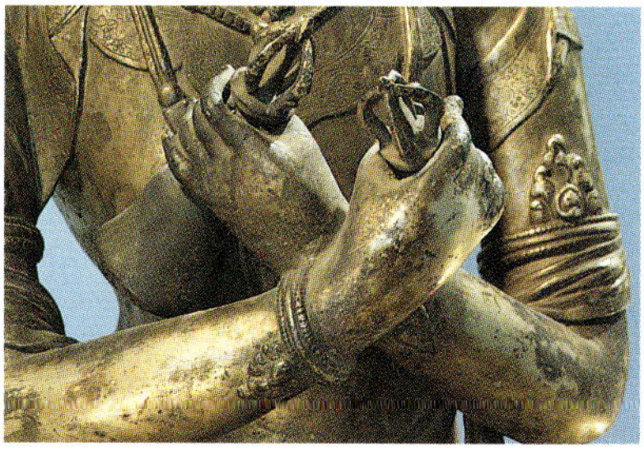

A 17th-century Tibetan statue of Vajra-Tara (female saviour) clasping two vajras.

THE *HEVAJRA TANTRA*

A great text of the Vajrayana is the *Hevajra Tantra* which explores the relationship of the male divinity Hevajra ("Ah *vajra*!") with his female partner Nairatmya (Not-self). A major purpose of this text is to unify perception of *samsara* (the cycle of rebirth) and *nirvana* (enlightenment). The apparent discrepancy between these realms lies in the identification of wisdom with *nirvana* and the "skilful means of compassion" with *samsara*. According to the *Hevajra*, only the rites contained in the Tantra will foster the view that "between *nirvana* and *samsara* there is not the slightest shade of difference … This essence which is Body, Speech and Mind of all the Buddhas is indivisible, and so known as *vajra*."

Hevajra embracing his female partner in vajra *or* yab-yum *attitude: "male" compassion joined with "female" wisdom.*

Besides such complex Tantric specialities, Tibetan adepts pursue their spiritual training on virtually the same lines as earlier Buddhist practitioners. They take refuge in the Three Jewels, practise tranquillity and insight meditation, contemplate the Four Truths, meditate on death and analyze the Three Marks of Existence (see pp.28–9). It is on this solid, orthodox foundation that further powers, derived from Tantra, are built.

Tantric deities

The Bon religion that the Tantric master Padmasambhava encountered when he arrived in Tibet in the 8th century AD (see pp.126–7) was preoccupied with deities and spirits who demanded, among other things, the blood sacrifice of animals. Rather than confront Bon practitioners with Buddhism as a power, Padmasambhava preferred to reconcile the *dharma* (Buddhist teaching) with the folk religion of the day. Perhaps the major example of agreement between Buddhism and Bon was the deal that was negotiated between Padmasambhava and Pe-har, the greatest of Tibet's national deities. According to legend, in return for renouncing his sacrificial demands, Pe-har acknowledged the protection of the *dharma*. And in lieu of blood, the god accepted, as a substitute offering, the egoism of the Tibetan people. This spectacular religious merge is typical of Tibetan *dharma* – most pre-Buddhist deities and demons of Tibet were either absorbed into Vajrayana or permitted to exist alongside the new religion.

A 17th-century Tibetan painting showing the bodhisattva *Manjushri seated on a lotus throne and surrounded by deities. Manjushri, after Avalokiteshvara, is the most popular Mahayana* bodhisattva. *Often depicted with a darkness-dispelling sword, he is shown here with the text of a* Prajnaparamita Sutra *above his left hand.*

An important aspect of the Vajrayana involves terrible deities. In the Hindu Tantra, the goddess Kali is the "black destroyer". Just as Kali represents the wrathful aspect of Shiva's consort Parvati, so "terrible" aspects of other Hindu deities were adopted by, or adapted to, the Tantric Buddhist pantheon. One example is Mahakala (Great Black One), a ferocious but protecting Buddhist deity who is a transformation of Shiva (see p.134). Fierce expressions of Buddhahood with up to twelve arms carrying various symbols such as drums, skull-caps and tridents are known as *herukas*. One such *heruka* is the deity Samvara: the ferocious aspect of the eastern heaven's benign *Jina* Buddha (see p.133). The *herukas* have wrathful consorts, known as *dakinis*, who are represented with dishevelled

An 18th-century votive plaque from Tibet, showing the ferocious deity Mahakala.

hair, a third eye and in dancing posture. Padmasambhava is believed to have received from *dakinis* the books on which he based his Tantric doctrine.

The benign *bodhisattvas* also have demonic emanations. The ferocious aspect of Manjushri, *bodhisattva* of wisdom, is Yamantaka (Conqueror of Death). According to one text, he should be depicted with "over-large head, scowling brows, three cruel eyes, a gaping mouth, canine fangs and rolling tongue". Another *Tantra* dictates that Yamantaka should be given a bull's head, and that his feet must trample animals and demons. The third eye, wild hair, skull-cap and trident are features of the god Shiva who likewise dances on the body of a defeated adversary, the personification of ignorance.

THE VISUALIZATION OF TUTELARY DEITIES

All Vajrayana practitioners have a tutelary deity or "god protector" (*yi-dam*) chosen for them as part of initiation by their teaching *lama*. The protector god is selected by the teacher to match the student's individual character. Each of the five celestial Buddhas has his wrathful *yi-dam*, and each of the *yi-dams* represents a psycho-spiritual defilement such as anger or hatred. In addition to the *yi-dam*, Tantric initiates receive a *mantra* associated with their god protector. Repeating their *mantra* with the help of a rosary, initiates learn to visualize their deity clearly. If the god represents the practitioner's special fault, then by conjuring the terrible and divine vision, he or she may start to transform a defilement into the virtue or wisdom embodied in the *yi-dam*'s corresponding opposite or benign manifestation. If, for example, the ferocious deity is Yamantaka, the practitioner under Yamantaka's tutelage will strive to acquire, and even become, the wisdom of the *bodhisattva* Manjushri. At its highest levels, the Tantric master (*siddha*) aspires, through rigorous mental yoga and in meditative trance, to identify with the highest possible tutelary deity. An important manifestation of the most sublime Buddha is Vajrasattva (*vajra* being) or Vajradhara (*vajra*-holder). Many of these supreme beings or their ferocious manifestations are also depicted embracing their consorts at the centre of *mandalas* (see pp.146–7). These are likewise vehicles by which the *siddha* realizes enlightenment through identification with the protective deity.

This 18th-century Tibetan statue shows Yamantaka (Destroyer of Death), an emanation of Manjushri, embracing female wisdom.

An 18th-century Tibetan statue of Vajrasattva in union with a Tara (female saviour) representing supreme wisdom.

Mandalas and *yantras*

Mandalas and *yantras* are ritual diagrams used in the Tantra and Tibetan *dharma* (doctrine), each being a symbolic miniature universe that serves as an object of meditation. These diagrams are of great antiquity, and the theory and techniques of *mandala* construction were transmitted from master to student in a continuous line; around the 11th century *mandala* meditation was introduced to Tibet from India. Today, *lamas* pass on their knowledge to initiates in the same way as they have done for centuries, and the present Dalai Lama, among others, continues this unbroken line of teaching.

A *mandala* is a sacred mansion, at the heart of which a deity resides, and the form of the Buddhist *mandala* derives in part from the design of Hindu temple architecture. A vital part of Hindu devotion is the contemplation of divine images, which lie deep within the temple, in the deity's sanctuary. Worshippers are drawn to this image: but progress through the temple is indirect. Moving through courtyards, past emblems of the god, its icons and symbolic animal, the devotee at last comes to the principal god's shrine and here, eye to eye (*darshana*), is absorbed into the divine presence.

The aim of the voyage through the temple is threefold. It signifies respect for the deity, acts as meditational preparation, and awakens a sense of manifold divine immanence. All the symbols enountered on the way toward the deity – with phenomena flowing in to the divine essence – represent components of a universe of which the god is the centre. On the return journey, the same symbols appear to flow out of the deity as elements of divine creation.

The practice of Tantra is different in many ways from Hindu temple practice – until recently available largely only to *brahmins*. Tantric devotion was traditionally held secretly among initiates of mixed caste; meetings often took place

A mandala *in the form of a shrine, showing Manjuvajra, a six-armed Tantric version of the* bodhisattva *Manjushri, with his* shakti.

A painted Shri Yantra from 18th-century Rajasthan. This classic Hindu pattern informs the symmetry of many Tibetan mandalas.

THE SHRI YANTRA

The archetypal *yantra* is the Shri Yantra, whose pattern evokes the sacred union of the goddess Shri with her partner, Shiva. The *yantra* is composed of three main elements. The outer framework is a square "shivered" or stepped to suggest the four doors of a sanctuary. Beyond these doors are the cardinal directions. Next is a series of concentric circles and petals representing the divine lotus of which the universe is a manifestation. Finally, at the centre, are nine interpenetrating triangles. The upward-pointing triangles represent the male god Shiva; those descending symbolize the female energy of the goddess (*shakti*). In the middle of the *yantra* lies an invisible dot (*bindu*): the absolute, graphically indescribable centre of power represented and created by conjoined female and male forces. Like a Hindu temple, the *yantra* demands a devotional journey inwards and then – once the divine presence has been encountered – out again. Again like the temple, the *yantra* is a miniature universe. Locked in its forms all worldly phenomena, evolving and dying, are evoked in the marriage of Shiva–*shakti*.

in areas chosen for their non-sacred, even polluted character. In the absence of temple architecture, a sacred area for the deity's residence was constructed in miniature. This sacred space might be traced on the earth with ground rice or shells, or more permanent diagrams cast in bronze, carved on rock or drawn on paper. These images are *yantras*, their geometric lines often being inscribed with *mantras* (auspicious syllables). These, together with the symmetrical quasi-architectural space that encloses the "inner sanctum" of the *yantra*'s pattern, evoke a sacred area in which to encounter a presiding deity.

The Dalai Lama marks guidelines for a sand mandala, *in a Vajrayana ritual. Sand* mandalas *are created in the spirit of non-attachment and, once made, are ritually destroyed.*

There are several levels of *mandala* ritual. At a rudimentary level, the *mandala* pattern, inscribed with auspicious syllables (*mantras* and *dharanis*), has long been used by Himalayan and Tibetan Buddhists as a magical talisman. Carried on the body in amulet cases, these charms were used for luck and good health or to defend their owners from natural and supernatural misfortune. At the level of monastic ritual, the construction of *mandalas* was, and continues to be, a daily event. Echoing the emperor Ashoka's thrice repeated "donation" of India to the Buddhist *sangha* (community), Tibetan *lamas* symbolically offer the entire universe, in the form of a *mandala*, to celestial Buddhas. They do this by tracing a *mandala* pattern with rice in four concentric rings round a circle representing Mount Meru (see pp.132–3). To accompany the *mandala* offering, the presiding *lama* enumerates the thirty-eight parts of the universe he has diagrammed and then offers them "to the gods of the *mandala* and the Buddhas and *bodhisattvas*". The formula ends with a prayer seeking the *Jina* Buddhas' protection and the purification of beings.

The *mandala* pattern was also used, from the earliest period of Tibetan Buddhism, on an altogether vaster scale. When the construction of Samye monastery southeast of Lhasa was started in the late 8th century AD (see p.127), pre-Buddhist deities were thought to have been angered by the implantation of Buddhism on their home territory. To pacify these local

A mandala, *ink on paper, from 9th-century T'ang China, showing the five Jina Buddhas with Vairocana at the centre.*

MANDALAS IN ARCHITECTURE

Yantra and *mandala* design originated in the structure of the universe as conceived by Hindu-Buddhist myth. At the centre of this mythic universe, holding its fabric together and surrounded by concentric rings of mountains and the four continents, stands Mount Meru, the cosmic axis (see pp.132–3). Much Hindu and Buddhist architecture is in a *mandala* form representing this cosmic pattern.

Like the monasteries of Tibet, the great Indian Buddhist reliquaries (*stupas*) such as those at Sanchi and Amaravati were also built to the pattern of the cosmic *mandala*: the floor of the dome having chambers clustered in rings around the central symbolic "world axis". A link between the human and universal was suggested by the Buddha himself: "A *stupa* is deserved by Awakened Ones, their disciples, and universal monarchs (*cakravartins*)."

Any monument with holy relics automatically becomes a symbolic axis mundi. Thus, like the Hindu devotee who moves clockwise through a temple toward the central shrine, the Buddhist pilgrim circumambulates a *stupa*'s *mandala*-like pattern. Wherever a *stupa* might be sited, it is, by virtue of its architectural form and holy contents, a universal centre.

spirits and create sacred Buddhist space, the Tantric master Padmasambhava drew on the earth a *mandala* of the five *Jina* Buddhas. On this *mandala*'s foundation, the monastery, itself in the shape of a *mandala* circle, was built.

The monasteries of Lhasa were likewise built in *mandala* pattern. At the centre of the pattern is the Dalai Lama's Potala palace. At the corners of an abstract square extending across Lhasa are the three other great monastic centres. The oldest and holiest of these is the Jokhang monastery, itself built on the "heart of a Demoness fallen on her back". This refers to a deity that represented the spiritual reality of pre-Buddhist Tibet. The monasteries built over her organs in Lhasa formed an imprisoning *mandala* which reached across Tibet, converting the whole of the nation to Buddhism.

Symbols of the *mandala*

The symbols of the *mandala* in Tibetan Buddhism are, at one extreme, cosmic, and at the other, intensely humanistic. At the universal extreme are representations of Mount Meru (see p.132) and celestial Buddhas; at the other are symbols of the human personality. A *mandala* is a meditational territory through which the initiate is invited to travel. This territory, organized with circles, lotus flowers, squares and other Buddhist symbols, is strictly ordered. Such symmetry may be described as a model of *nirvana*: flawless and eternal.

But implicit within this perfection are suggestions of *samsara*: the realm of change, suffering, human ordinariness and moral imperfection. This is the realm of personal experience – the world as it is understood by the meditator who gazes into the *mandala*'s labyrinth. The eloquence of *mandala* symbolism lies in just this tension between *samsara* and the *nirvanic* ideal. If we did not live in *samsara* what need would we have for *nirvana*; if *nirvana* did not exist, how should we be able to identify the problem of *samsara*?

The *mandala*, then, may be seen as a double mirror. On the one hand it reflects, in the meditator's gaze, the face of *samsara*. On the other hand it holds signs of a truer reality which, in the earlier stages of spiritual development, are beyond comprehension. Enlightenment is achieved when the meditator arrives at a complete understanding of the first factor of the Eightfold Path: "right view" (see p.25). In most Tibetan Tantric schools, this is the view that sees *nirvana* in *samsara*: the essential oneness of all realms in Buddhahood. At this point the poles of *mandala* symbolism converge. The meditator's "mirrored" personality, with all its samsaric defilements, is seen simply as a component of the nirvanic totality: the wisdom and compassion expressed by the Buddha at the centre of the pattern.

A late 19th- or 20th-century hanging silk Tibetan thanka *(cloth painting) showing the* Jina *Buddha Vairocana's emanation, Sarvavid (All Knowing), surrounded by the figures of nine deities,* bodhisattvas *and worshipping* lamas.

A 20th-century depiction, in the Tibetan style, of the five Jina *Buddhas painted in their symbolic colours.*

SYMBOLS OF *SAMSARA*

Immediately identifiable aspects of *samsara* are the "terrible" aspects of the Buddhas and *bodhisattvas*, at least one of which will be the subject of the initiant's regular meditation (see p.141). In the Tibetan Buddhist tradition, the early stages of *mandala* meditation are always supervised by a teaching *lama* who will choose for the student a *mandala* governed by one of the five *Jina* Buddhas (see p.133) whose terrible manifestation corresponds to the student's principal fault.

All humans are seen as belonging to a "family" corresponding to one of the *Jina* Buddhas; and each of these families is represented by one of five spiritual faults: delusion, anger, greed, envy or ill-will. The number five is further represented in the pattern: each of the five factors of personality (*skandhas*, see pp.28–9) is linked both to a fault and a symbolic colour. The personality factors are symbolized and metaphysically associated as shown in the table below.

At the centre of the *mandala* sits an image of a sublime or wrathful Buddha or one of the Buddhas embracing his consort (see pp.137, 141). Moving toward the *mandala*'s centre, and confronting their own defilements in the shape of demons and the terrible aspects of their family Buddha, meditators will survey a complex of both impersonal and subjective symbols.

Contemplation of a *mandala* is not isolated from the rest of the meditator's practice. As the personality becomes free of its faults and the *skandhas* cease clinging to the notion of an ego, then the *mandala*'s symbols begin to converge. Images of *samsara* become one with *nirvana*. The meditator's negative projections – represented by the wrathful *Jina* – are absorbed in the infinite, central, compassionate Buddha.

Buddha	Colour	*Skandha*	Fault
Vairocana	White	Form	Delusion
Ratnasambhava	Yellow	Feeling	Ill-will
Amitabha	Red	Consciousness	Greed
Amoghavajra	Green	Karmic deposits	Envy
Aksobya	Blue	Perception	Anger

Buddhism Comes to the West

The first reference by a European to Buddhism came from the Venetian, Marco Polo, who saw miracle-working monks ("idolators" as he called them) at the court of Kublai Khan in the 13th century. A long non-Buddhist silence followed. Then in the mid-19th century Mahayana manuscripts from Tibet and Nepal reached London and Paris and, in parallel, palm-leaf books from Sri Lanka and Burma brought the Theravada canon to Europe.

Initial linguistic and historical interest in Buddhism was soon complemented by an interest in the content of the *dharma* (doctrine). Nurtured by organizations like the London Buddhist Society and by visiting Oriental teachers, Buddhist practice in Europe and North America was, on a small but secure scale, established by the late 1930s. The 1960s was a time of both advance and confusion. While many seekers burned out on fringe spirituality, others who committed themselves to Buddhist ideas spent time in the East, and returned to Europe and North America to join communities. Since the 1970s these centres have grown in size and number. The presence in the West of Oriental masters, made possible by post-war affluence and easy intercontinental travel, has always been vital.

A monk meditating at Chithurst monastery, England. The sangha *affirms that monastic life is far from being a retreat from the world. Monks and nuns are engaged in teaching and environmental conservation in addition to a routine devoted to* vipassana *(insight), meditation and an authentic Theravada discipline.*

The early European linguists

Europe's discovery of Buddhism stemmed from the study of Sanskrit and Tibetan by travellers and colonial administrators who worked in India and Tibet in the 18th and 19th centuries. Pre-eminent among the Sanskritists was the English scholar Sir William Jones, who, in his spare time from the Bengal judiciary, established the Asiatick Society of Bengal and published *Asiatick Researches*, the first European journal devoted to Oriental studies. Support came from Warren Hastings, India's governor-general, who had encouraged Charles Wilkins to translate the Hindu *Bhagavad Gita* (1783). Three years later, Sir William Jones announced his astonishing comparison of the Sanskrit, Latin and Greek languages. The fact that the three ancient tongues had such similar grammars could not, argued Jones, "possibly have been produced by accident".

An engraving from a medallion depicting French scholar Eugène Burnouf.

Besides this momentous discovery, Sir William's major works were translations of the Hindu *Laws of Manu* and the classical Sanskrit play *Shakuntala*. It was then only a matter of time before Europeans devoted to Oriental texts a similar degree of scholarly attention as they gave to the European classics.

The study of languages was soon followed by a passion for collecting manuscripts. One important collection of Buddhist texts was assembled in Nepal during the 1820s by the Englishman Brian Hodgson, which he dispatched to London, Oxford and Paris. Another was material collected by Alexander Csoma de Koros, who spent many years studying Mahayana texts in Tibetan monasteries.

The Sanskrit manuscripts Hodgson sent to Paris found their way to a scholar ideally suited to their complexities: Eugène Burnouf (1801–52), who

EUROPEAN SCHOLARS AND MONKS

Many Europeans became convinced Buddhists as well as scholars. One, the German Paul Dahlke, established a meditation centre in Berlin-Frohnau in 1922, and the house continues today as the headquarters of the German Dhammaduta Society.

Perhaps the most influential scholar-practitioner was Anton Gueth, a concert violinist, who entered a Sri Lankan monastery in 1903, taking the monastic name Nyanatiloka (Knower of Three Worlds). In 1911, he established the Island Hermitage, a retreat for scholar monks in Sri Lanka, and there wrote some of the most influential European books on Theravada. Among his students were the distinguished European monks Nyanaponika and Nanamoli, both of whom contributed to the canon of modern Buddhism with important commentaries and translations.

The Singhalese abbot of the Island Hermitage meditating on human bones. The hermitage was established by Nyanatiloka near the village of Dodanduwa in Sri Lanka.

T.W. and Caroline Rhys Davids, co-founders of the Pali Text Society, with friends and family in an English garden.

with his knowledge of Sanskrit, Pali and Tibetan, was the first European to appreciate the vast extent of Buddhist culture. Burnouf's great contributions were his *L'Introduction à l'histoire du bouddhisme indien*, and his translation of the *Lotus Sutra*, both of which opened a way into Buddhism for scholars and amateur Orientalists alike.

Burnouf's students at the Collège de France continued his monumental work of editing and translating Buddhist texts, and strong English, German, Russian and Danish philological traditions had developed by the 1880s. A European demand for good reading texts was met by two enterprises. One was the Sacred Books of the East, published by Max Muller, which presented annotated English translations of Hindu and Buddhist scriptures, many of which are in print today. The second was the Pali Text Society (PTS), co-founded in 1881 by Muller with T.W. and Caroline Rhys Davids. T.W. Rhys Davids had learned Pali in Sri Lanka and he returned to England with palm-leaf manuscripts of the complete Pali *Tri-pitaka* (see p.71). Over the next forty years, the PTS published virtually the whole Pali canon, and this work continues, with new editions still appearing.

Nineteenth-century Orientalism

This painting of the Buddha, by the French artist Odilon Redon (1840–1916), exemplifies the influence of Oriental themes and ideas on 19th-century artists in Europe.

European interest in Oriental cultures had its prelude in a long association with the Judaeo-Christian vision. But Orientals of post-biblical literature, such as Shakespeare's Shylock or the Islamic knights of Edmund Spenser's *Faerie Queen*, were often sinister figures. That almost every character in the Bible was Jewish was a fact too anthropologically remote to have much bearing. Shakespeare's Othello, a Muslim convert to Christianity, is a heroic, if ambiguous, exception.

In the late 18th century, the yearning for absolute symbols transcended the embattled Judaeo-Christian ideal and grasped the Oriental as its focus. For most writers, this image, derived largely from travel writing, had a poetic and/or erotic content. Coleridge's dream, in 1797, of Kubla Khan's "pleasure dome" is of a languorous Oriental paradise. Episodes in Byron's *Don Juan* (*c.*1819) contain comic Levantine harem fantasies. In 1814 Goethe began studying Persian poetry and created the mystical and erotic dialogues of the *East-West Divan*. "The leaf of this tree, entrusted to my garden from the east, offers the experience of secret meaning," opens one of these great lyrics. Goethe knew little of Buddhism, but the sentiment and imagery express a European receptivity to ideas from the East.

In the 19th century it was the literary theorist Friedrich von Schlegel, together with the philosopher Arthur Schopenhauer, who most enthusiastically embraced Hindu-Buddhist ideas. Like the Romantic poets, these writers had few Oriental texts to rely on and no first-hand experience. But both Schlegel and Schopenhauer had read translations of the Hindu religious texts the *Bhagavad Gita* and the *Upanishads*, and both were conversant with 18th-century linguistic scholarship. "In the Orient we must see the highest Romanticism," proclaimed Schlegel in 1800, and in *On the Language and Wisdom of Indians* he wrote: "May Indic studies find as many disciples and protectors as Germany and Italy saw spring up in such great numbers for Greek studies in the 15th and 16th centuries…"

Schopenhauer's book *The World as Will and Representation* owed much both to the philosophy of Kant and to a mix of Hindu and Buddhist notions.

THE LIGHT OF ASIA

One of the Sanskrit texts translated into English in the mid-19th century was the *Lalitavistara*, a poetic account of the Buddha's youth and enlightenment. Using a prose translation of this work, Sir Edwin Arnold, an English poet who had travelled in India, wrote a long verse narrative which was published in 1879 as *The Light of Asia*. Arnold's poem created an immediate interest in Buddhism in Victorian England and North America. By one of the ironies of British colonial history, this vastly successful poem helped re-establish Buddhism among the literate classes of 19th-century Sri Lanka who had been alienated from their native religion.

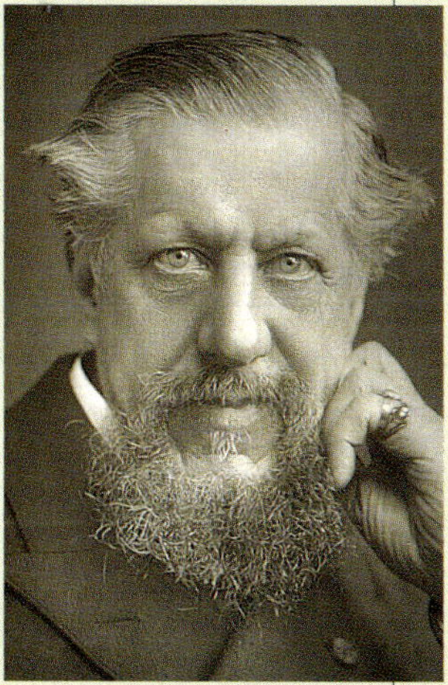

Sir Edwin Arnold (1832–1904), author of The Light of Asia, *photographed in 1893.*

Life, argued Schopenhauer, is governed by an aimless and unconscious force that he described as "will". Unconscious of their thraldom to the unknowable will, "people succumbed to an innate but deluded realism that drove them to achieve unattainable goals, such as happiness in this world. Schopenhauer believed that the purposeless striving of the will could be suspended through contemplation of music and art and ultimately transcended through mystical intuition" (Batchelor, 1994).

By the mid-1850s, Schopenhauer had read the works of Burnouf (see pp.150–51) and he was able to tie his ideas more closely to Buddhism. "You will arrive at Nirvana," he wrote, "where you will no longer find these four things: birth, old age, sickness and death… Never has myth come closer to the truth nor will it." In a late version of *The World as Will*, he wrote that the suspension of the will would in its essence "be identical with the Nirvana of the Buddhists".

A page from the sketchbook of Lt. John Henry Bagnold, who served in the Indian army in the early 19th century. This sketch is of a seated Buddha at Sanchi, including architectural details, and is copiously annotated by the artist.

Buddhism in modern Europe

Although Buddhism came to the West in the 19th century, today's Buddhist communities in Europe are a relatively new phenomenon. When the English Buddhist Society was established in 1924, its purpose was: "To publish and make known the principles of Buddhism, and to encourage the study and practice of these principles." Visiting Oriental teachers such as D.T. Suzuki provided authenticating support to its meetings, and writers like Christmas Humphreys and Edward Conze wrote works of continuing influence. For more than seventy years, from its London premises, the Buddhist Society has published books, run courses and summer schools and conducted training in meditation.

While Buddhist life in Asia has always radiated from the *sangha*, the notion of a European monastic community was almost unthinkable until the late 1960s. Then came a watershed with the explosion into European consciousness – an aspect, perhaps, of liberation politics and psychedelic anti-reason – of Eastern spirituality. The first communities grew up in the 1960s, but it took some years for the movement to consolidate. Inspired by the adventurous *Zeitgeist* of the 1960s, US Peace Corps idealism and even Hermann Hesse's fiction, travellers who had been in the East returned to Europe and North America. In jungle huts and rural monasteries, contending with heat, flies, solitude and often hunger, they had meditated, cleared paths, washed latrines, learned difficult languages and schooled themselves to Buddhist discipline. These new "white Buddhists" talked not of drugs and guru magicians but of long, detailed *dharma* study. The re-entry in the 1970s of this scattering of initiates coincided with the arrival in Europe of Asian teachers. Some came on teaching visits; a few established communities of monks, nuns and lay people of both European and Oriental origin. These Buddhist centres, where lay people lived under the guidance of *dharma* masters, were new to Buddhist history.

THERAVADA, ZEN AND THE FBO

Perhaps the most influential European to be trained in the East in the 1960s was Ajahn Sumedho, who established the Amaravati Buddhist monastery. Ordained in Thailand by the late Thai master Ajahn Chah, the American-born *bhikkhu* co-founded a small Theravada monastery in London in 1977, and the next year moved to Chithurst in Sussex. A second centre, Amaravati, for monks, nuns and laity, was established in Hertfordshire in 1984. Combining an authentic Theravada discipline with friendliness and good humour, this *sangha*'s influence has spread to Europe, America and Australasia. Supported by the English Sangha Trust and by lay donations, monks and nuns enjoy a strong relationship of reciprocity with individuals on residential retreats and with groups which host teaching visits from the *sangha*.

In the absence of a major Japanese community in Europe, Zen is less well established there than it is in the United States. But courses in Zen meditation are offered by the London Buddhist Society, and also, notably, at Throssel Hole Priory: a Soto Zen community for both monastic and lay training in Northumberland established in 1972 by Reverend Master Jiyu-Kennett.

The Friends of the Western Buddhist Order (FBO), another influential Buddhist *sangha*, was established in 1967 by Ven. Sangharashita, an Englishman who spent more than twenty years studying and teaching in India.

SAMYE LING

A number of *lamas* exiled from Tibet settled in Europe in the 1960s and 1970s. Some re-created their own monastic groups in France, Switzerland and Spain, others formed mixed communities of monks and laity. The oldest and largest of these, co-founded in 1967 by Akong Tulku Rinpoche and Chogyam Trungpa Rinpoche, is Samye Ling in southeast Scotland. Named after the ancient Tibetan Samye monastery, Samye Ling follows the Kargyu tradition established by Marpa (see p.130). Daily meditation lies at the heart of its practice; at its most rigorous this involves ten years' training, including a three-year retreat at Samye Ling's new centre on Holy Island off the west coast of Scotland. At the mainland centre, residents and visitors follow a broad-based complex of Buddhist discipline. Practical work as an expression of generosity and mindfulness is part of the daily routine, the most visible result being the completion in 1988, after ten years' labour, of the temple. The study of Tibetan *dharma*, language and medicine are other major offerings.

Samye Ling also reaches into the contemporary world. Inter-faith symposia are a means of achieving mutual understanding with other religions. New forms of therapy have been developed, and Akong Rinpoche has established ROKPA, a charitable programme with aid projects in Tibet and Nepal as well as among the homeless in England and Scotland.

Dharma *students meditate and chant in the shrine room at Samye Ling with its exquisitely finished wooden panelling.*

Monks on retreat on Holy Island cultivating their vegetable garden. Practical work has often been part of Tibetan Buddhist routine.

Residents of Samye Ling who have studied Tibetan iconography in depth become trained artists in the Tibetan tradition.

North American mystics

American poet Walt Whitman (1818–92).

Three great 19th-century writers, Emerson, Thoreau and Whitman, were the major voices heralding the entry of Indian mysticism to North America. Wilkins's *Bhagavad Gita* (see p.150) reached Emerson and Thoreau in the mid-1840s, and *The Light of Asia* was greeted by their friend Oliver Wendell Holmes as "so lofty that there is nothing with which to compare it but the New Testament". It was Thoreau who first introduced a Buddhist text to the American public. Having read Burnouf's *Introduction to Indian Buddhism* (see pp.150–51), he translated sections of the *Lotus Sutra* from French and in 1844 published them in *The Dial*.

However, more significant than his translations is Thoreau's famous account of his contemplative solitude at Walden Pond: "I love a broad margin to my life. Sometimes, in a summer morning ... I sat in my sunny doorway from sunrise till noon, rapt in reverie, amidst the pines and hickories and sumachs, in undisturbed solitude and stillness ... I grew in those seasons like corn in the night ... I understand what the Orientals mean by contemplation and the forsaking of works..." (*Walden*, 1854). Few European or North American writers have come closer than this to the non-grasping dynamic of Buddhistic consciousness.

Walt Whitman was also inspired by texts from India. While Thoreau's meditation has a Theravada-like quietism, an aloofness from society, Whitman's poetry, shamanistic, animistic and Hindu by turns, expresses an all-embracing quasi-Mahayanist affinity for his companions in the creation. "I am the mate and companion of people," he proclaims in *Song of Myself*. And enamoured of both the uniqueness and equality of all beings, his imagination courses like a *bodhisattva* through the cosmos, fervently celebrating all he encounters, whether it is wild geese, grass, black slaves, boot-soles, the President or the "commonest, cheapest". At first cheerfully denying that he had read Indian scriptures, Whitman calls, in *Passage to India*, for a return to the "primal thought of old occult Brahma ... and the tender junior Buddha". It is of course unnecessary to describe Thoreau or Whitman as "Buddhist". Touched only marginally by the Buddha's doctrine, each expresses a temper of mind to which Buddhism aspires.

THE FIRST NORTH AMERICAN BUDDHIST

The first American Buddhist was probably Colonel Henry Steel Olcott (1832–1907), co-founder with Helena Blavatsky (1831–91) of the Theosophical Society, a spiritualist movement somewhat misleadingly known as "Esoteric Buddhism". On a visit to Sri Lanka in 1880, Olcott and Blavatsky participated in one of the great moments in modern Buddhism. At a temple in the port of Galle, the two "white Buddhists" knelt before a monk, repeated the Five Precepts (see p.57) and took refuge in the Three Jewels (see p.41). No Oriental had ever witnessed Europeans submitting to the Buddhist faith. And thus began Olcott's commitment to Buddhism which immeasurably nourished the revival of Buddhism in colonized Sri Lanka.

ABOVE Colonel H.S. Olcott, who helped establish three colleges and 250 schools to further Buddhist education in Sri Lanka.
LEFT H.P. Blavatsky: unlike Olcott, she never forsook the occult in favour of Buddhism.

THE WORLD'S PARLIAMENT OF RELIGIONS IN CHICAGO

North Americans saw their first "official" Buddhists at the World's Parliament of Religions in Chicago in 1893. Here, alongside the Japanese Zen monk Soyen Shaku, Colonel Olcott's colleague Anagarika Dharmapala from Sri Lanka delivered two famous and impassioned lectures.

This encounter in North America between Oriental Buddhists and Europeans led to important developments. Buddhism found a friend in the voice of writer and publisher Paul Carus of LaSalle, Illinois. Moreover, at the end of the Parliament, Mr C.T. Strauss, a New York businessman, took refuge in the Three Jewels (see p.41), and was thus the first American to be "admitted to the faith of Buddha" on US soil. Also attending the conference was a student of Soyen Shaku. This was D.T. Suzuki, whose writings would become central to the growth of Zen in America.

Buddhism in modern North America

Buddhism in modern North America has two very different main constituencies. There are the Chinese, Japanese, and more recently, southeast Asian communities with temples in American cities where Buddhist practice is often based on different forms of Pure Land *dharma* (see pp.92–3, 108–9). The other main constituency consists of European American Buddhists and their Oriental meditation masters.

North America has long been the resort of Eastern scholars and teachers. Ananda Coomaraswamy (1877–1947) wrote many of his important works at the Indian department of the Boston Museum. D.T. Suzuki taught intermittently for many years at Columbia University, where the composer John Cage and the writers Alan Watts and Allen Ginsberg were among his students. A great deal of the strength of North American Buddhism derives from such cultural interaction, which in the past fifty years has slowly generated stable, confident Buddhist institutions. Given that "beat Zen" in the 1950s was often an expression of postwar spiritual angst and anomie, it is an extraordinary achievement that authentic Zen, Tibetan and, more lately, Theravada cultures into which many Americans have moved since the 1970s, have rendered the psycho-social alienation of the educated middle classes less of an issue.

Two *dharma* masters who were crucial to the acculturation of Buddhism in North America were Shunryu Suzuki-roshi and his successor Katagiri-roshi who came to the United States in 1958 and founded the San Francisco Zen Center, with its farm and mountain retreat in northern California. Another important teacher is the Korean Zen master Seung Sahn, who established the first of his own centres in Providence, Rhode Island, in the 1960s. These teachers, among others, taught long enough to give rise to American Zen lineages. And since American Zennists have an affinity with the lovely ritual trappings of Japanese Zen, meditation in Zen environments adds aesthetic pleasure to the quest for *satori* (Zen enlightenment).

ABOVE *Shunryu Suzuki-roshi, founder of the San Francisco Zen Center.*
LEFT *The dormitory in the San Francisco Zen Center.*

ZEN AND THE TIBETAN *DHARMA*

Of the many high *lamas* who fled persecution in Tibet, a significant number settled in North America. The late Chogyam Trungpa Rinpoche established centres in Colorado, Vermont and Nova Scotia. Students of Trungpa in recently renamed Shambhala centres now form a worldwide organization. Writers such as Anne Waldman, Allen Ginsberg and John Giorno teach alongside Buddhist specialists at the Naropa Institute in Colorado, another branch of Shambhala's activity.

The beauty and complexity of the Tibetan *dharma* has also stimulated many American Buddhists to become scholars, eroding the boundaries between academic life and *dharmic* practice. Jeffrey Hopkins, whose early studies were at the Lamaist Buddhist Monastery of America, is HH Dalai Lama's official interpreter. Robert Thurman studied in many Tibetan monasteries and disrobed to become an academic writer.

Buddhism informs the work of a number of American poets. Allen Ginsberg, Jack Kerouac, Gary Snyder and Philip Whalen discovered Buddhism in the mid-1950s. Snyder and Whalen lived and studied in Japanese Zen monasteries; Snyder's work is informed by *dharmic* environmentalism, and Whalen, now a Zen monk, writes in a unique American Zen idiom.

Since the late 1960s, there have been important large-scale American Buddhist publishing ventures. Tarthang Tulku, founder of Berkeley's Nyingma Institute, set up Dharma Publishing in 1968. Huge numbers of translated commentaries and texts have issued, since the 1970s, from Wisdom Publications and Shambhala.

THERAVADA IN NORTH AMERICA

Theravada Buddhism took root in North America during the 1970s significantly under the guidance of Joseph Goldstein and Jack Kornfield, who returned from training in the *dharma* (the Buddhist path) in India and Thailand respectively. Goldstein studied in Bodh Gaya with Anagarika Munindra, a Theravada scholar and teacher, and returned to the United States to co-found the Insight Meditation Center in Barre, Massachusetts. Based in Theravada, Goldstein's book *The Experience of Insight* (1976) reflects a deep, non-sectarian realization of the *dharma* as a whole. Jack Kornfield has also written a number of influential books, and has developed a fusion of Buddhist teaching and Western psychotherapy.

Another influential master is the Singhalese *bhikkhu* Henepola Gunaratana, who has established communities in Washington D.C. and Virginia. Visits to North America from English *bhikkhus* for retreats and conferences have further helped to develop Theravada philosophy and practice in North America.

Non-sectarian in its affiliation, the American Buddhist review Tricycle *publishes a wealth of information on contemporary Buddhist practice.*

Documentary Reference

Selected Buddhist sites

INDIA

Bodh Gaya (Bihar)
Before his death, the Buddha enjoined his followers to make pilgrimages to four sites: Lumbini, where he was born; Uruvela (modern Bodh Gaya), the site of his enlightenment; Sarnath, the place of his first sermon; and Kushinara, where he died. Each of these sites may be visited today, and Bodh Gaya remains the most sacred of the four.

After the decline of Indian Buddhism in the 12th century, most Buddhist sites were destroyed or fell into disrepair. In 1891 the Sri Lankan Anagarika Dharmapala founded the Mahabodhi Society, which set out to reclaim Bodh Gaya for Buddhism; this was achieved in 1949. Bodh Gaya today is a busy centre of pilgrimage with monasteries and meditation centres run by Tibetan, Burmese, Thai and Vietnamese communities. Visitors will see a remote descendant of the *bodhi* tree, the magnificent but greatly restored 7th-century Mahabodhi temple (see p.25), the Buddha's stone seat (*vajra-asana*) and a museum of Buddhist and Hindu materials.

Yambulakang monastery near Tsethang, Tibet, is the oldest building in the country.

Sarnath (Uttar Pradesh)
The Deer Park at Sarnath just north of Varanasi was the site of the Buddha's first discourse and today contains some of the most impressive Buddhist monuments in India. The beautiful park is dominated by the 5th-century Dhamekh *stupa*: one of two *stupas* marking the spot where the Buddha is said to have preached. The remains of smaller *stupas*, shrines, five monasteries and the lower half of an inscribed Ashokan column are among other monuments to have been excavated since the 19th century.

Sarnath's archeological museum contains the Ashokan column's famous lion capital (emblem of the modern Indian state; see p.59) and many other important works in stone, including a sublime figure of the teaching Buddha from the Gupta period (5th century). Like Bodh Gaya, Sarnath has a thriving international Buddhist community.

Sanchi (Madhya Pradesh)
Perhaps the finest and most complete Buddhist monument in India is Sanchi's great *stupa* with its four magnificent free-standing gates (*toranas*). The vast brick *stupa* itself dates from around the 3rd century BC, but its carved gates and railings were probably executed two centuries later during the Satavahana dynasty. Sanchi was excavated in the early 19th century, and the restoration of the site by British and French archeologists was initiated in 1912.

Visitors today, like traditional Buddhist worshippers, can

circumambulate the *stupa* in a clockwise direction and contemplate the teeming sculptural forms that fill the gate-posts and their lofty architraves. *Jataka* narratives (see p.22), hieratic elephants and royal lions, Hindu-Buddhist deities and exquisite female nature spirits crowd every part of the four *toranas*. The small archeological museum houses excavated sculptures; other important Sanchi pieces are in museums in Delhi, London and Los Angeles.

Ajanta (Maharashtra)
The wild, crescent-shaped ravine pierced with more than twenty Buddhist cave temples makes this one of India's most spectacular sites. Many genres of early medieval sacred art, from elaborately carved monastic halls, to sculptures and wall paintings, are represented here, and prominent among Ajanta's glories are murals painted in glowing reds, blues and greens. Unique to Indian Buddhist tradition, the paintings, in high Gupta style, furnish a vision of Mahayana generosity: a mingling of human, divine and natural forms in a suspension of warm and life-enhancing interplay.

Most sublime in grace, compassion and serenity is the incomparable figure of Padmapani, the lotus-carrying aspect of the *bodhisattva* Avalokiteshvara (cave 1). Scenes from *Jataka* narratives adorn the walls of several other monasteries in the complex.

NEPAL

Kapilavastu and Lumbini
Siddhartha Gautama, the future Buddha, was born at Lumbini near the Shakyan capital of Kapilavastu in the southern region of Nepal known as the *terai* (see map on p.34). The 5th-century Chinese pilgrim Fa-hsien described Kapilavastu as a "great scene of empty desolation", populated by a few monks, a score or two of families and dangerous animals such as lions and white elephants. Fa-hsien none the less visited well-known sites, including the Shakyan palace, the place where the child *bodhisattva*'s identifying marks were discovered, and, east of the city, the garden of Lumbini where the future Buddha's mother bathed and gave birth. Mounds, *stupas* and other ruins testified to previous Buddhist institutional prosperity. Buddhist tradition tells that the emperor Ashoka visited Nepal in the 3rd century BC and erected a *stupa* and an inscribed column at Lumbini. Recent excavations have uncovered evidence of *stupas*, monastic dwellings and the well-preserved structure of the bathing-pool. The Ashokan column – rediscovered in 1896 but snapped in half by a lightning bolt – may also be seen at Lumbini. Theravada and Tibetan monasteries have been built in the past two decades near Lumbini, re-establishing the site as an important, although geographically remote, devotional centre.

The Svayambhunath stupa *at Kathmandu.*

Svayambhunath and Bodhnath (Kathmandu)
To commemorate his missionary visit, the emperor Ashoka is said to have built innumerable *stupas* in Nepal. Two surviving examples, much restored, may derive from the Ashokan period. These are the remarkable Svayambhunath and Bodhnath *stupas* in Kathmandu. Both *stupas* share unique Nepalese

architectural features. Surmounting the conventional dome is a "steeple" raised on thirteen diminishing tiers to symbolize the thirteen Buddhist heavens. Yet more striking is the design of the square base (*harmika*) from which the tiers rise. The *harmika* is gilded, and a face gazes with immense eyes of inlaid metal and ivory from each side. One explanation for this unique Nepalese iconography is that the eyes suggest a solar cult expressed on some Hindu temples by "sun-faces". A second idea is that the temple represents the "primal man" (*mahapurusha*) of early Hinduism. Buddhist theory would suggest that the eyes are a sign of the "all-seeing" Buddha. Visitors are certainly struck by the way in which the eyes follow them as they move round the *stupa* precincts.

SRI LANKA

Anuradhapura (north-central Sri Lanka)

Today's Anuradhapura is a huge park containing the ruins of the Great Monastery (Mahavihara; see p.68) established *c.*250BC on the outskirts of the ancient Singhalese capital. Anuradhapura is connected by an eight-mile (13km) pilgrim's path to Mihintale where the missionary Mahinda first preached and where an excavated *stupa* can be visited (see p.68). Disinterred earlier this century from the jungle growth of more than a millennium, Anuradhapura's *stupas*, monastic ruins, sculptures, reservoirs, and a possible descendant of the original *bodhi* tree, provide an intense experience of ancient Buddhism. Dominating the site are two vast *stupas* with characteristic Singhalese "bubble domes". The Thuparama, although much restored, is probably the oldest monument in either India or Sri Lanka. The Ruwanweli Dagaba, is also heavily restored, and is clad in the undecorated white plaster which differentiates Singhalese *stupa* architecture from the more ornate Indian style.

At Anuradhapura a wonderful convergence of the modern and the archaic may be experienced. On May and June full moon days, the festivals of Wesak and Poson celebrate, respectively, the Buddha's birth, enlightenment and *parinirvana*, and the introduction of Buddhism to Sri Lanka. At such festivals, Anuradhapura is enlivened by hundreds of thousands of devotees. For the modern-day visitor, one of the great pleasures is touring Anuradhapura on a rented bicycle.

Polonnaruwa (northeastern Sri Lanka)

While Anuradhapura evokes the austerity of early Singhalese Buddhism, the later site of Polonnaruwa, wonderfully situated on Lake Topawewa, offers an unparalleled view of medieval Buddhist sculpture and architecture. There the visitor may see the immense recumbent *parinirvana* Buddha and the 25-foot (7.5m) rock-cut figure of Ananda standing by the head of the Master (see p.32). There too is the colossal meditating Buddha (see p.27), and the famous sculptured portrait of the sage-king Parakramabahu overlooking the lake and in contemplation of a manuscript.

Equally dazzling are the early 13th-century monuments situated on the "Great Quadrangle". These include the classically proportioned pyramidal brick *stupa* (Sat Mahal Pasada), the carved stonework of the "temple of the tooth relic" (not to be confused with the Temple of the Tooth in Kandy) and the waving lotus-stem-shaped columns of the Nissanka Lata Mandapaya.

Just as Anuradhapura was abandoned by the 8th century, Polonnaruwa was finally conquered by the Tamils in the 15th century. The art of Polonnaruwa represents the final flowering of Singhalese Buddhist art, still matchlessly preserved in land-locked jungle.

THAILAND

Bangkok and Ayutthaya

Some of the oldest and best-preserved stupas *in Thailand are at Ayutthaya.*

Much important early and medieval Thai architecture was ruined in southeast Asian wars, but impressive 19th- and 20th-century Buddhist temples abound in Thailand, and in many parts of the country there are lovely archeological sites. In Bangkok, the Wat Phra Kaeo temple, built by King Rama I (1782–1809) in the precincts of his Grand Palace, is a spectacular monument to the Theravada Buddhist revival initiated in the 19th century. This temple is a centre of Thailand's religious life, symbolizing the close bond between *sangha* (religious community) and state, and houses the "Emerald Buddha", a figurine of national importance to modern Thai people.

The southern Thai Ayutthaya period of the 14th to 18th centuries brought an influx of new architectural ideas from Sri Lanka. Perhaps the most beautifully preserved of Thailand's medieval monuments are at the Ayutthaya historical park, north of Bangkok. Of special interest are *stupas* with characteristic Thai "lotus bud" domes, and temple towers showing the influence both of medieval Khmer design and of "honeycombed" south Indian *shikhara* towers.

CAMBODIA

Angkor Thom and the Bayon Temple

After a horrifying period of war, the Hindu temple complex of Angkor Wat and the Buddhist Angkor Thom are again accessible. Angkor Thom was the creation of the Khmer "god-king" Jayavarman VII (1181–1219), who converted to Mahayana following the destruction of Angkor by the Cham (Vietnamese) during his father's reign. Jayavarman's Buddhism seems to have been a revised version of the Brahmanical religion which previous Khmer kings had exploited to deify their own persons. The central deity in Jayavarman's religion was Lokeshvara, "Lord of the Worlds", and rebuilding Angkor Thom on a stupendously grand scale, the king created a "Buddhist" city as a monument to Lokeshvara, who was an aspect of Jayavarman's divine self. This convergence of king and deity is still visible in the portrait masks of Jayavarman carved on the four faces of the Bayon temple towers of Angkor Thom.

Like Borobudur (see p.77) and many other southeast Asian temples, Angkor Thom was conceived as a model of the Buddhist universe. At the centre of an immense complex of shrines is the great Bayon temple with its cluster of five towers, the tallest of which represents Mount Meru, the cosmic axis (see p.132). The whole of Angkor was moated with 100 yards (90m) of water and criss-crossed by a brilliantly engineered system of canals: the water motif symbolizing the cosmic ocean and the world's four sacred rivers and – not least – acting as an irrigation system. Much of the power of Angkor Thom emanates from a profusion of hybridized

Hindu-Buddhist iconography, carved in a wild, sweet style on the gates and terraces of Jayavarman's temple-mountain. The god-king's portrait gazing across his shattered domain adds sinister pathos.

A view of the 13th-century Bayon temple, Angkor Thom.

TIBET

Lhasa

Visitors may currently enter Tibet from mainland China, Hong Kong or Nepal, if they have a visa for China; the Chinese authorities maintain "closed" areas, but most of the country is accessible. In the holy city of Lhasa, the Dalai Lama's Potala Palace, like many Tibetan monasteries, is now a state museum. Unlike countless shrines and monasteries destroyed during the Cultural Revolution, both the structure and contents of the Potala are preserved. Symbol of the protection of Avalokiteshvara and of the greater Tibetan Buddhist community, the Potala still towers imposingly over Lhasa, and contains countless treasures from the 17th century, including murals, *thankas*, *mandalas*, altars, and the famous statue in sandalwood of Padmapani.

The Jokhang monastery, southeast of the Potala, is the most sacred of all Tibetan pilgrimage sites. Somehow surviving the barbarities of the Cultural Revolution, the Jokhang retains its famous gilded roof, and the "Four Deities Radiating Light" may still be seen in their shrine. The Jokhang remains a living monastery; but it may also be visited, like other sacred sites, as a "museum".

CHINA

Yung-kang (Shansi) and Lung-men (Honan) caves

Yung-kang is one of the most remarkable Buddhist sites for the massive simplicity of its immense rock-carved Buddhas and the delicate ornamentation of its narrative reliefs. Work on the cave shrines was started by the emperor of the first Wei dynasty in AD460, in response to persecution of Buddhists over the previous twenty years. In the next decades, in the limestone river cliffs at Lung-men (5th–6th centuries), Wei dynasty monumental carving achieved a spiritual and aesthetic perfection never repeated. The giant Buddhas at Yung-kang recall Indian prototypes; at Lung-men early Buddhist and Mahayana motifs converge in a graceful, serene and authentically Chinese idiom.

JAPAN

Nara and Kyoto

Nara, the Japanese imperial capital in the 8th century, remains one of the great centres of East Asian Buddhist history. In and around Nara's historic park are pagodas, early Buddhist and Shinto shrines, formal gardens, the important Nara National Museum, and not least the Todai-ji temple with its immense bronze Buddha statue.

The beauty of old Kyoto lies in its numerous Zen temples dating from the Hieian period, and the famous gardens – "hill gardens" featuring water, and dry gardens featuring rock and sand – of temples such as Tenryu-ji and Ryoan-ji. Zen is a living tradition and Western students are accepted at some temples in Kyoto as well as in many of the more remote monasteries in the north of the island.

Four great modern masters

VENERABLE THICH NHAT HANH (BORN 1926)

Venerable Thich Nhat Hanh was one of the leaders of the Vietnamese peace movement and a co-founder of the Tiep Hien ("inter-being") order, a group of monks engaged, at constant personal risk, in helping victims of the Vietnamese war. Author of many books and a member of the Buddhist Peace Delegation in Paris, Nhat Hanh emerged as an international figure in 1966, when he toured the United States in an effort to "describe the agony of the voiceless Vietnamese people".

Nhat Hanh has been as much a spokesman against Soviet and South African oppression and the nuclear arms race as against the crimes committed in his own country, and his Buddhism is rooted in classic mindfulness practice.

"Our daily lives," says Nhat Hanh, "the way we eat, drink, walk, all has to do with the world situation. Meditation is to see deeply into things, to see how we can change, how we can transform the situation."

Thich Nhat Hanh currently lives in France, where he teaches and gardens at his Plum Village community.

ZEN MASTER SEUNG SAHN (BORN 1927)

Ordained as a Zen monk in 1948, Seung Sahn served five years in the South Korean army and spent nine years teaching in Japan before moving to the West in 1972. Initially supporting himself on the east coast of the United States as a laundromat technician, Seung Sahn established a Zen centre at Providence, Rhode Island, and this now has many branches throughout the United States and Europe.

Seung Sahn is presently one of the best-known and most powerful teachers in the Buddhist world. Speaking in the recognizably challenging style of the Zen patriarchs, Seung Sahn communicates in a voice which is at once learned, orthodox and dazzlingly fresh. Transcripts of his talks and letters are filled with a *dharma* which is wonderfully alive and deeply lived. Students of Zen and Mahayana texts such as the *Heart Sutra* and the *Diamond Sutra* will find the quintessential Mahayana position spontaneously elaborated in much of Master Seung Sahn's teaching.

"Is the *bodhisattva* attached to compassion?" asks a student; to which Seung Sahn's response is: "The universe is infinite. A *bodhisattva* attachment is no attachment. No attachment is a *bodhisattva* attachment."

Or: "You say in your letter," writes Seung Sahn, "'The sky is bluer after the rain, and the sunshine falls brightly.' This is a very good sentence, but there is a pitfall in it. Please try to find this pitfall."
(From *Dropping Ashes on the Buddha*, Grove Press, 1976.)

VENERABLE MAHA GHOSANANDA (BORN 1929)

Few countries are in greater need of healing leadership than Cambodia, where millions continue to be victims of more than twenty years of war, Khmer Rouge atrocities and now the weakness of an often corrupt government. Working within this context is Maha Ghosananda, who was nominated for the 1994 Nobel Peace Prize.

During the Khmer Rouge reign of terror in the mid-1970s when monks were being executed and monasteries and Buddhist monuments closed and desecrated, Maha Ghosananda, in common with millions of his compatriots, lost virtually all his own kin. When

Thailand's border with Cambodia was invaded by "walking skeletons" in flight from Khmer Rouge terror, Maha Ghosananda established Buddhist temples in the refugee camps, and built into his teaching a Buddhist compassion which opened for victims the possibility both of psychological survival and of forgiveness. Maha Ghosananda brought the same message of reconciliation and non-violence to Khmer Rouge refugees who filled the same camps in the late 1970s.

He continues his work of peace and rehabilitation today, with a special remit from the government for essential aspects of environmental reconstruction.

TENZIN GYATSO, THE FOURTEENTH DALAI LAMA (BORN 1935)

Recognized at the age of two as the incarnation of the previous Dalai Lama, and enthroned at the age of five, the present, fourteenth Dalai Lama undertook monastic training at Tibet's Buddhist universities and assumed temporal power in 1951 – the year in which China extended its authority over the country.

The Chinese invasion, followed by the popular uprising in Lhasa in 1959, which the Chinese brutally crushed, led to the almost total destruction of Tibet's religious community. Some 80,000 refugees fled across the borders to India. The Dalai Lama, too, left Tibet, and established a Tibetan community in Dharamsala, north India.

Tirelessly active on behalf of contemporary global welfare in addition to that of his own nation, and deeply learned in esoteric Buddhism, the Dalai Lama, in his life and teachings, both exemplifies the *bodhisattva*'s vow (see pp.60–61) and lends reality to the notion of his own ancestry as an incarnation of Avalokiteshvara. (For a history of the lineage of the Dalai Lamas, see pp.130–131.)

The Dalai Lama is the author of numerous books, including *My Land and My People*; *Kindness, Clarity and Insight*; and *The Meaning of Life from a Buddhist Perspective*. He was awarded the Nobel Peace prize in 1989.

The fourteenth Dalai Lama is perhaps the first and only Buddhist master to achieve international celebrity. Instantly recognizable from innumerable media images, the Dalai Lama projects a happiness and modesty which make him one of the best-loved 20th-century public figures. Exiled head of a devastated nation, his Holiness is honoured for his life-long devotion to his people and for a compassion that transcends his own tragic status. The uninformed platitude that Buddhists are absorbed by suffering is belied by the Dalai Lama's manifest delight in life. One may sense in this photograph that the enthroned leader is also bowing.

Map of Asia

This map is intended as a general geographical reference and as a guide to places of importance in the Buddhist world that are mentioned in the book. The names and geographical borders on the map are not intended as an accurate portrayal of present-day political realities.

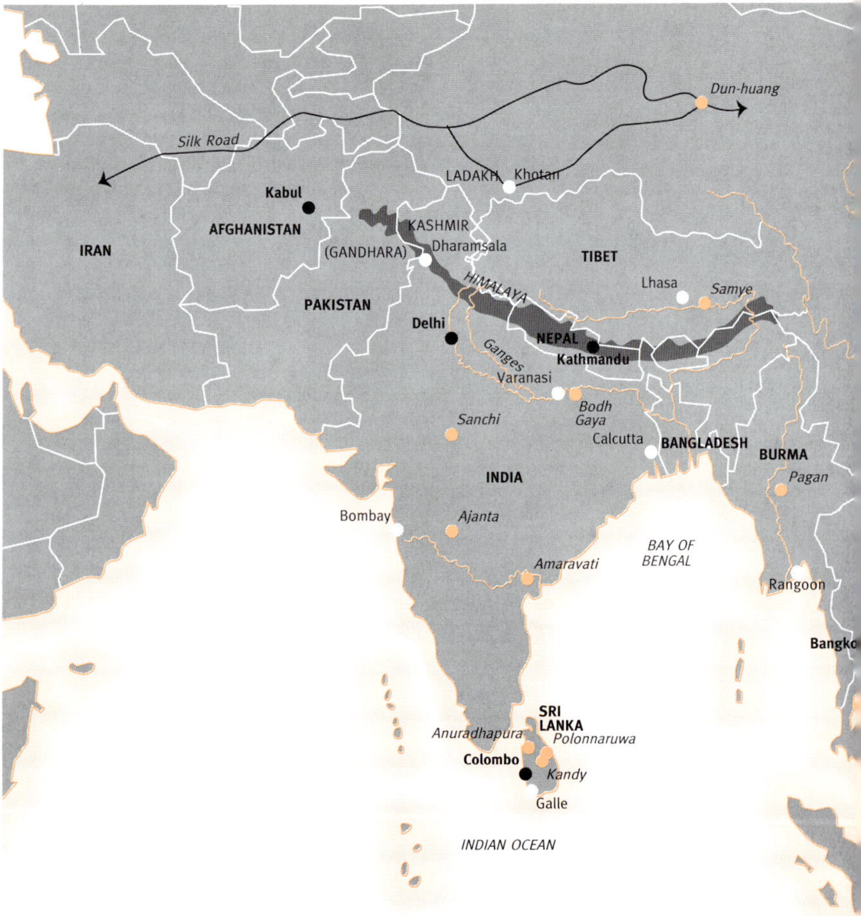

Beijing
Yung-kang
KOREA
JAPAN
HINA
Huang-He
Kyoto
Tokyo
Kamakura
Nara
Lung-men
SOUTH CHINA
SEA
PHILIPPINES
VIETNAM
Ho Chi Minh
BORNEO
Chandi
Mendut
Borobudur
JAVA
Towns and Cities
Capital cities
Buddhist sites
KASHMIR Regions

Useful addresses

THERAVADA

Insight Meditation Society
1230 Pleasant Street
Barre, MA 01005
USA
(508) 355 4378

Theravada Buddhist Meditation
IMC-USA
438 Bankard Road
Westminster, MD 21158
USA
(410) 346 7889

Amaravati Buddhist Centre
Great Gaddesden
Hemel Hempstead
Herts HP1 3BZ
UK
(01442) 842 455

The Buddhist Village Trust for Sri Lanka
34 Glover Road
Pinner
Middlesex HA5 1LG
UK
(0181) 868 1446

Chithurst Buddhist Monastery
Chithurst
Petersfield
Hants GU31 5EU
UK
(01730) 814 986

International Meditation Centre
Splatts House
Heddington, Calne
Wiltshire SN11 OPE
UK
(01380) 850238

London Buddhist Vihara
5 Heathfield Gardens
London W4 4JU
UK
(0181) 995 9493

Pali Text Society
73 Lime Walk
Headington
Oxford OX3 7AD
UK

Buddhist Publication Society
54 Sangharaja Mawatha
P.O. Box 61
Kandy
Sri Lanka

Mahasi Centre
16 Thathana Yeiktha Road
Rangoon
Burma

Wat Pa Nanachat
Bahn Bung Wai
Amper Warin
Ubon 34310
Thailand

TIBETAN

Karme-Choeling
Buddhist and Shambhala Meditation Centre
Barnet, Vermont 05821
USA
(802) 633 2384

Rigpe Dorje Center
P.O. Box 690995
San Antonio, TX 78269
USA
(210) 698 0529

Sang-ngak-cho-dzong
P.O. Box 247
Chelsea Station
New York, NY 10113
USA
(212) 439 4780

Dharmadhatu (Chogyam Trungpa organization)
27 Belmont Close
London SW4
UK
(0171) 720 3207

Jamyang Meditation Centre
10 Finsbury Park Road
London N4 2JZ
UK
(0171) 359 1394

Kagyu Samye-Ling Tibetan Centre
Eskdalemuir
via Langholm
Dumfries DG13 0QL
UK

Manjushri Institute (Geshe Kelsang Gyatso)
Conishead Priory
Ulverston
Cumbria LA12 9QQ
UK
(0229) 54029

Marpa House
Rectory Lane
Ashdon
Saffron Walden
Essex CB10 2HJ
UK
(079984) 415

Tashi Khyil Tibetan Buddhist Centre
54 Derryboye Road
Crossgar
Co. Down BT30 9LJ
UK

The Tibetan Foundation
10 Bloomsbury Way
London WC1A 2SH
UK
(0171) 404 2889

Karma Kagyu Ling
St. Léon-sur-Vezère
F-24290 Montignac
France

Osel Ling
Bubión
E-18412 Granada
Spain

Tharpa Choeling
CH-1801
Mont Pélérin ZE1
Switzerland

Tibetisches Zentrum e.V.
Hamburg
Hermann-Balkstr 106
D-2000 Hamburg 73
Germany

Vajradhatu Europe (Chogyam Trungpa organization)
Zwetschenweg 23
D-3550 Marburg
Germany

Office of HH the Dalai Lama of Tibet
Thekchen Choeling
McLeod Ganj
Dharamsala, Himachal Pradesh
India

ZEN

Honolulu Diamond Sangha Training Committee
Palolo Zen Center
2747 Waiomao Road
Honolulu, HI 96816
USA
(808) 735 1347

Minnesota Zen Meditation Center
3343 East Calhoun Parkway
Minneapolis, MN 55408
USA
(612) 822 5313

San Francisco Zen Center
300 Page Street
San Francisco, CA 94102
USA
(415) 863 3136

Zen Center of Los Angeles
923 South Normandie Avenue
Los Angeles, CA 90006-1301
USA
(213) 387 2351

Zen Community of New York
21 Park Avenue
Yonkers, NY 10703
USA
(914) 376 3900

London Zen Society
10 Belmont St.
London NW1 8HH
UK
(0171) 485 9576

GENERAL

Angulimala, the Buddhist Prison Chaplaincy Organization
The Forest Hermitage
Lower Fulbrook
Warwick CV85 8AS
UK
(01926) 624885

The Buddhist Society
58 Eccleston Square
London SW1V 1PH
UK
(0171) 834 5858

The London Buddhist Centre
51 Roman Road
London E2 OHU
UK
(0181) 981 1225

Nichiren Shoshu UK
UK Headquarters
1 The Green
Richmond
Surrey TW9 1PL
UK

Sharpham North Community
Ashprington, Totnes
S. Devon TQ9 7UT
UK
(0803) 732 542

Vietnamese Buddhist Society in UK
Linh-Son Temple
89 Bromley Rd.
London SE6 2UF
UK
(0181) 461 1887

Wisdom Books Ltd.
402 Hoe Street
London E17 9AA
UK
(0181) 520 5588

Boeddistische Unie van Nederland
Shetlands 6, 3524 ED
Utrecht
The Netherlands

Buddhistisches Haus
Edelhofdamm 54
D-1000
Berlin 48
Germany

Centre for Coordinating Buddhist Groups
c/o Aleksandr Breslavetz
Kuntsechoinei Datsan
91 Primorsky Prospekt
St. Petersburg
Russia 197228

Commaunité Bouddhique de France
Taikan Jyoji Roshi
La Rialle
F-07800 St. Laurent du Pape
France

Deutsche Buddhistische Union
Ana Rosia Findeisen (Vive-President)
Scheideweg 3
D-2000 Hamburg 20
Germany

Thich Nhat Hanh
Plum Village
Meyrac
Boubes, Bernac
F-47120 Duras
France

Unione Buddhista Italiana
c/o Istituto Lama Tzong Khapa
via Poggiberna 5
I-56040 Pomala (Pisa)
Italy

Buddhist Federation of Australia
Box 161, Holme Building
University of Sydney
NSW 2006
Australia

World Fellowship of Buddhists
33 Sukhumvit Road
Bangkok 10110
Thailand

Glossary

Abhidhamma (Pali), ***Abhidharma*** (Sanskrit) Analysis of *Dharma* or Further *Dharma*, one of the three *pitakas* of the Pali scriptures

Adi Buddha the supreme, primordial Buddha in the Tantric *dharma*

ahimsa non-harming, non-violence

alaya-vijnana the "store consciousness" of Yogacara theory

Amitabha the Buddha presiding over the western paradise in Pure Land Buddhism

anatta (Pali), **anatman** (Sanskrit) the doctrine of not-self; with *dukkha* (suffering) and *anicca* (impermanence), one of the "three marks of existence"

anicca (Pali) impermanence

arhat enlightened person who has obliterated defilements, extinguished craving and achieved *nirvana*

aryan noble; often used to describe high doctrine such as the Four Noble Truths, or a spiritual aristocrat

Avalokiteshvara Mahayana *bodhisattva* of compassion, central to Tibetan *dharma*

bhikkhu (Pali), **bhikshu** (Sanskrit) literally "beggar"; Buddhist mendicant, monk

bodhi enlightenment, realization; describes the tree under which the Buddha achieved enlightenment in 531BC

bodhisattva in Hinayana a future Buddha; in Mahayana an "enlightenment being" who strives to lead others to *nirvana*

Bon pre-Buddhist Tibetan religion

Brahma the first of the three major Hindu deities

Brahman Sanskrit term for Hindu absolute spirit

brahmin member of the priestly caste

Buddha awakened, enlightened; the historical figure Siddhartha Gautama (566–486BC), the enlightened one of the present era

Buddhism path and practice based on teachings of the Buddha (the Buddha, however, taught *dharma*)

cakravartin legendary universal emperor

cetiya "reminder" of the Buddha in *stupa* form

Ch'an non-ritualistic school of Chinese Mahayana emphasizing the direct experience of reality in meditation

cha-no-yu the Japanese tea ceremony

deva deity; often a relatively minor spiritual being

dhamma (Pali), **dharma** (Sanskrit) Buddhist teaching; "what is"; mental or material phenomenon

Dharma-kaya the ultimate Buddha in Mahayana metaphysics

dukkha suffering, unhappiness; dissatisfaction. "Birth, old age, death, grief, lamentation, discomfort, unhappiness, despair, the wish for something unobtainable, the five clinging constituents of personality are all *dukkha*" (*Digha-Nikaya* II 305)

Gautama (Sanskrit), **Gotama** (Pali) Siddhartha's clan name

Ge-lugs-pa the Dalai Lama's school of Tibetan Buddhism

guru spiritual teacher

heruka fierce expression of Buddhahood in the Tantra

Hevajra a male divinity in the Tantra

Hinayana the "Small Vehicle": a term given by the Mahayanists to those who were alleged to seek enlightenment for themselves rather than for others

Jataka Buddhist birth story

jhana meditative absorption

Jina "conqueror" Buddha, of whom there are five, each dwelling in one of the heavens of Vajrayana Buddhism

kami Japanese Shinto deity

karma work, action, self-inherited accumulation of past actions

koan Zen conundrum used for meditation

kshatriya Indian warrior caste

Kuan Yin Chinese for Avalokiteshvara

Madhyamika "those who take the Middle Way": a school of Mahayana

Mahamaya Siddhartha's mother

Mahavamsa ancient Sri Lankan chronicle

Mahavihara the Great Monastery near Anuradhapura, Sri Lanka

Mahayana the "Great Vehicle" school of Buddhism, so called because it carries many to *nirvana*

mandala circle, meditative pattern, magical diagram representing consciousness and the cosmos

Manjushri a *bodhisattva* who cuts through ignorance

mantra sacred syllable used in meditation

Mara the evil one, tempter

Muchalinda infernal serpent king (*naga*) who shielded the Buddha during his enlightenment meditation

mudra ritual or meditational hand gesture

naga serpent king or deity

namo homage: used in the important Theravada formula

Namo tassa bhagavato arahato samma sambuddhassa: "Homage to the blessed one, the worthy one, the completely enlightened one"
Nembutsu homage formula in Japanese Pure Land
nirvana a blowing out, extinction of self, the condition of enlightenment
Om universal mantra
Pali language of southern Buddhism into which the Theravada scriptures were translated in 5th-century AD Sri Lanka
parinirvana complete *nirvana*, the Buddha's condition of death
Parvati Hindu goddess, Shiva's consort or *shakti*
Patimokha monastic rules set out in the *Vinaya* section of the Pali scriptures
pipal tree *Ficus religiosus*, the *bodhi* tree under which the Buddha was enlightened
pitaka "basket" or body of texts in the Pali scriptures; the three *pitakas* are *Suttas* (Discourses), *Vinaya* (Monastic Discipline) and *Abhidhamma* (Further *Dharma*)
prajna special knowledge, wisdom
Prajnaparamita perfection of wisdom, a class of Mahayana text elaborating the doctrine of *shunyata* (emptiness); the goddess embodying the doctrine
puja ritual offering; worship
punna merit accumulated by a blameless life and good works, and leading to favourable rebirth
samadhi concentration, inner unification
samsara round of rebirths, the realm of unsatisfactoriness; in Theravada the opposite of *nirvana*; Mahayana teaches the ultimate equality of *samsara* and *nirvana*
sangha the Buddha's community, and all subsequent monastic groups
Sanskrit literary and sacred language of ancient India, the language of many Mahayana texts
sasana Buddhist teaching
satori experience of Zen enlightenment
shakti divine female energy
Shakyamuni Sage of the Shakyas, a name for the Buddha
shaman mystical adept specializing in spirit flight
Shingon Japanese "esoteric Buddhism"
Shiva one of the three major Hindu deities
shunyata emptiness, the Mahayana Buddhist absolute
siddha spiritual adept in the Tantra
Siddhartha the Buddha's personal name
sima monastic boundary within which ordination may take place
skandha "heap", five of which constitute a human being
stupa dome-shaped Buddhist reliquary
sutra (Sanskrit), **sutta** (Pali) Buddhist discourse
Tantra esoteric Hindu or Buddhist text; a late school of the Mahayana that heavily influenced Tibetan Buddhism
tao "the way", ultimate reality in Chinese Taoism
Tara "female saviour", a female deity in Mahayana
tathagata the "thus-gone" or "thus-come": the Buddha
tathata "thusness, suchness": reality as conceived by the Mahayanist Yogacara school
Theravada Doctrine of the Elders, major school of southern Hinayana
Ti-pitaka (Pali), ***Tri-pitaka*** (Sanskrit) the "three baskets" of texts in the Pali scriptures: *Suttas, Vinaya, Abhidhamma*
Ti-ratana (Pali), **Tri-ratana** (Sanskrit) the Three Jewels or Gems of Buddhism: Buddha, *dharma, sangha*
upasaka lay disciple
upaya the "skilful means" of compassion often associated in Tantric Buddhism with a male Buddha working in conjunction with the female principle of *prajna* (wisdom)
Vairocana one of the *Jina* Buddhas, important to Japanese Shingon and Tantric practice
vajra thunderbolt or diamond; a Mahayana symbol of the absolute
Vajrayana the vehicle of the *vajra*, the Tibetan Mahayana tradition
vassa the Indian rainy season
Veda ancient Hindu text
Vinaya code of Buddhist monastic discipline, as set down in Pali, and in Chinese and Tibetan translations from Sanskrit
vipassana literally "special, intensive, multi-directional seeing"; insight meditation
yantra sacred diagram
yi-dam tutelary deity in Tantric *dharma*
Yogacara idealistic school of Mahayana elaborated in the *Lankavatara Sutra* and in the works of Asanga and Vasubhandu
yogi a spiritual practitioner, a term used most in Hindu and Tibetan Buddhist traditions
zazen Zen meditation
Zen Japanese for Ch'an: the "school of meditation"

Further reading

This list is confined largely to books published or reprinted in the past twenty years.

Basham, A.L. *The Wonder that was India* (Grove Press, New York, 1959) Sidgwick & Jackson, London, 1985

Batchelor, S. *The Awakening of the West*, Aquarian, Harper Collins, London 1994

Bechert, H. and Gombrich, R. eds. *The World of Buddhism*, Thames & Hudson, London & New York, 1984

Carrithers, M. *The Buddha*, Oxford University Press, Oxford, 1983

Ch'en, K. *Buddhism in China*, Princeton University Press, 1973

Conze, E. ed. *Buddhist Texts through the Ages*, Harper & Row, New York, 1964

Conze, E. ed. *Buddhist Scriptures*, Penguin, London and New York, 1973

Coomaraswamy, A. *History of Indian and Indonesian Art*, Dover, New York, 1988

de Bary, T. ed. *Sources of Japanese Tradition*, Columbia University Press, New York, 1958

de Bary, T. ed. *Sources of Chinese Tradition*, Columbia University Press, New York, 1960

Dowman, K. *The Power-Places of Central Tibet*, Routledge, London, 1988

Dumoulin, H. ed. *Buddhism in the Modern World*, Collier Macmillan, London, 1976

Dumoulin, H. *Zen Buddhism – A History*, Collier Macmillan, New York & London, 1988

Eliade, M. ed. *The Encyclopedia of Religion*, Macmillan, New York, 1987

Fields, R. *How the Swans Came to the Lake*, Shambhala, Boston & London, 1986

Freemantle, F. and Trungpa, C. *Tibetan Book of the Dead*, Shambhala, Boulder, Colorado, 1978

Getty, A. *The Gods of Northern Buddhism*, Dover, New York, 1988

Gombrich, R. *Theravada Buddhism, A Social History from ancient Benares to modern Colombo*, London, 1988

Goldstein, J. and Kornfield, J. *Seeking the Heart of Wisdom*, Shambhala, Boston, 1988

Harvey, P. *An Introduction to Buddhism*, Cambridge University Press, 1993

Johansson, R.E.A. *Pali Buddhist Texts Explained to the Beginner*, Curzon Press, London, 1977

Kitagawa, J.M. *Religion in Japanese History*, Columbia University Press, New York, 1966

Kitagawa, J.M. ed. *Buddhism and Asian History*, Macmillan, New York, 1989

Ling, T. *The Buddha*, Penguin, London & New York, 1973

Michell, G. *Penguin Guide to the Monuments of India*, London & New York, 1989

Murti, T.R.V. *The Central Philosophy of Buddhism*, Unwin, London, 1980

Nyanaponika Thera, *The Heart of Buddhist Meditation*, Weiser, New York, 1971

Nyanatiloka Thera, *Buddhist Dictionary*, Buddhist Text Society, Kandy, Sri Lanka, 1986

Rahula, W. *What the Buddha Taught*, Wisdom Books, London, 1990

Rawson, P. *The Art of Southeast Asia*, Thames & Hudson, London, 1993

Rowland, B. *The Art and Architecture of India*, Penguin, London, 1971

Snellgrove, D. *Indo-Tibetan Buddhism: Indian Buddhists and their Tibetan Successors*, Serindia, London, 1987

Snelling, J. *The Buddhist Handbook*, Rider, London, 1988

Stanley-Baker, J. *Japanese Art*, Thames & Hudson, London, 1991

Suzuki, D.T. *An Introduction to Zen Buddhism*, Rider, London, 1983

Suzuki S. *Zen Mind, Beginner's Mind*, Weatherhill, New York, 1972

Tharpar, R. *A History of India, vol.1*, Penguin, London & New York, 1974

Thomas, E.J. *The Life of the Buddha*, Routledge, London, 1975

Tucci, G. *The Religions of Tibet*, University of California Press, Berkeley, 1980

Tucci, G. *The Theory & Practice of the Mandala*, Rider, New York, 1974

Tworkov, H. *Zen in America, the Search for an American Buddhism*, Kodansha, 1994

Warder, A.K. *Introduction to Pali*, Pali Text Society, Oxford, 1963

Warder, A.K. *Indian Buddhism*, Motilal Banarsidass, Delhi, 1980

Warren, H.C. *Buddhism in Translations*, Atheneum, New York, 1979

Whitfield, R. and Farrer, A. *Caves of the Thousand Buddhas, Chinese Art from the Silk Route*, British Museum Publications, London, 1990

Wright, A.F. *Buddhism in Chinese History*, Stanford University Press, 1959

Yokoi, Y. *Zen Master Dogen*, Weatherhill, New York & Tokyo, 1976

Zwalf, W. ed. *Buddhism: Art and Faith*, British Museum Publications, London, 1985

Index

Page numbers indicate a reference in the main text. There may be references in captions or feature boxes on the same page. Page numbers in *italic* indicate a reference in an illustration caption only. Page numbers in **bold** indicate a reference in a feature box.

A

B

C

D

N

O

P

W

Y

Z

Picture credits

The publisher thanks the photographers and organizations for their kind permission to reproduce the following photographs in this book:

Abbreviations
A above; **C** centre; **B** below; **L** left; **R** right
AA&A: Ancient Art and Architecture Collection
BAL: Bridgeman Art Library
RHPL: Robert Harding Picture Library
V&A: Victoria and Albert Museum
PP: Panos Pictures

1 Alain de Gardmeur/PP; **2** Jean-Leo Dugast/PP; **7** Hutchison Library

The Early Days of the Buddha
8–9 Ann and Bury Peerless; **10** Jean-Loup Charmet; **11AL** C.M. Dixon; **11AR** A&B Peerless; **11B** Musée Guimet/RHPL; **12A** Musée Guimet/e.t. archive; **12B** Ann and Bury Peerless; **13** Ann and Bury Peerless; **14** C.M. Dixon; **15** V&A/Michael Holford; **17B** J. Holmes/PP

The Enlightenment
18–19 Cliff Venner/PP; **20** AA&A ; **21** RHPL; **22** National Museum of India, New Delhi/BAL; **23A** British Museum/OMPB 13538; **24** RHPL; **25** Ann and Bury Peerless; **26** RHPL; **26–7** British Museum; **27** Hans Hinz; **28–9** AA&A; **29** RHPL; **30** Hutchison Library; **31** Hutchison Library

From Enlightenment to Death
32–3 David Beatty/RHPL; **34** AA&A; **35** U Ba Kyi, Burmese Buddhist Temple, Singapore; **36–7** Ann and Bury Peerless; **38A** A&B Peerless; **38B** AA&A; **39** J.H.C. Wilson/RHPL; **40A** British Library/OR12010/J; **40B** National Museum of Bangkok/RHPL; **41** Jean-Leo Dugast/PP; **42** British Museum; **42–3** British Museum; **43** British Library/OR14298 F24-25; **44BL** Dr Nigel Smith/Hutchison Library; **44BR** Jon Spaull/PP; **45A** Joth Shakerley/PP; **45C** Ann and Bury Peerless; **46** Ann and Bury Peerless; **47** Ann and Bury Peerless; **48** Ann and Bury Peerless; **49A** British Library/OR14298; **49B** British Museum/C.M. Dixon; **50–51** Ann and Bury Peerless

Early Indian and Mahayana Buddhism
52–3 RHPL; **54** Philip Goldman Collection/Werner Forman Archive; **55A** British Museum; **55B** Hans Hinz; **56** Hans Hinz; **57** Jean-Leo Dugast/PP; **58** Ann and Bury Peerless; **59A** Michael Holford; **59B** e.t. archive; **60–61** J.H.C. Wilson/RHPL; **62** British Museum/Michael Holford; **63** RHPL; **64A** Ann and Bury Peerless; **64B** AA&A; **65** AA&A

Theravada or Southern Buddhism
66–7 Werner Forman Archive; **68** C.M. Dixon; **69A** RHPL; **70A** Jean-Leo Dugast/PP; **70B** C.M. Dixon; **71A** J. Holmes/PP; **71B** British Museum/OR5340 a&b; **72A** RHPL; **72BR** Graham Harrison; **72BL** Graham Harrison; **72–3** Graham Harrison; **74** Jean-Leo Dugast/PP; **75** Jean-Leo Dugast/PP; **76** Graham Harrison; **77A** B. Barbey/Magnum; **77B** Graham Harrison

Buddhism in China
78–9 AA&A ; **80A** British Museum/RHPL; **81A** British Museum/C.M. Dixon; **81BL** AA&A; **81BR** Michael Holford; **82** AA&A; **83A** Jean-Loup Charmet; **83B** Werner Forman Archive; **84** Oriental Museum, Durham University/BAL; **85A** e.t. archive; **85B** Jean-Loup Charmet; **86** Bibliotheque Nationale, Paris/BAL; **87** Bibliotheque Nationale, Paris/BAL; **88** British Museum; **89A** British Museum/RHPL; **89B** e.t. archive; **90** AA&A; **91** British Library/OR8210/S6983; **92A** British Museum; **92B** British Museum/BAL; **93** British Library/BAL; **94** Freer Gallery/RHPL; **95** Eisei Bunko Foundation, Tokyo; **96** Museum of Antiquities, Stockholm/RHPL; **97** Christie's Colour Library

Buddhism in Japan
98–9 Images; **100A** RHPL; **100B** Hutchison Library; **101** J. Holmes/PP; **102A** Douglas Dickens; **102B** British Library/OR764-60; **103** Werner Forman Archive; **104A** AA&A; **104B** S. McBride/RHPL; **105** British Library/OMPB 16107.q.36; **106** British Library/OMPB 16006.e.30; **107** British Library; **108** British Library; **109** British Museum/RHPL; **110** AA&A; **111** British Library; **112A** British Museum/RHPL; **112B** Douglas Dickens; **113** e.t. archive; **115** Eisei Bunko Foundation, Tokyo; **116** Graham Harrison; **117** RHPL; **118A** RHPL; **118B** Graham Harrison; **119A** RHPL; **119B** Graham Harrison; **120** Hutchison Library; **121A** Michael Holford; **121B** Graham Harrison; **122** Private Collection/Werner Forman Archive

Buddhism in Tibet
124–5 RHPL; **126** Gavin Heller/RHPL; **127A**

Michael Holford; **127B** Philip Goldman Collection/Werner Forman Archive; **128** Alain Le Gardmeur/PP; **129** RHPL; **130B** Neil Cooper/PP; **131A** Felix Greene/Hutchison Library; **131B** AA&A; **132** V&A/e.t. archive; **133** Oriental Museum, Durham University/BAL; **134B** Ann and Bury Peerless; **134–5** V&A/e.t. archive; **135B** RHPL; **136** V&A/Michael Holford; **137** Jean-Loup Charmet; **138** Chester Beatty Collection, Dublin; **139CL** Philip Goldman Collection/ Werner Forman Archive; **139CR** Musée Guimet/ Michael Holford; **140A** AA&A; **140B** V&A/BAL; **141** Philip Goldman Collection/Werner Forman Archive; **142** AA&A; **143** Neil Cooper/PP; **145** British Museum/Stein Collection/0173; **146** Oriental Museum, Durham University/BAL; **147** Andy Weber/Tharpa Publications

Buddhism Comes to the West
148–9 Graham Harrison; **150A** MEPL; **150** Graham Harrison; **151** Pali Text Society, Oxford; **152** Musée d'Orsay, Paris/BAL; **153A** Mary Evans Picture Library; **153B** Royal Asiatic Society, London; **155** Nigel Howard **156** Mary Evans Picture Library; **157** Mary Evans Picture Library; **158** Los Angeles Zen Center, San Francisco; **159** Tricycle Review/New York

Documentary Reference
160 RHPL; **162** Hutchison Library; **165** Hutchison Library; **166** Neil Cooper/PP

Every effort has been made to trace copyright holders. However, if there are any omissions we would be happy to insert them in future editions.

Pali and Sanskrit translations are by the author.

FOR ANNA SAMARUNA KAMALA